Take a Bite of Eternal Life

Volume II

By Michael F. Blume

Take a Bite of Eternal Life
Volume II

By Michael F. Blume

Copyright ©2012 Michael F. Blume

Third Printing 2012

Cover Design by Michael F. Blume

Edited by Shelley Phillips

All Scripture quotations in this book are from the *King James Version* of the Bible unless otherwise indicated.

All rights reserved. No portion of this publication may be reproduced, stored in electronic system, or transmitted in any form or by any means, electronic, mechanical, photocopy, recording or otherwise, without the prior permission of Michael F. Blume. Brief quotations may be used in literary reviews.

For additional copies see:
THAT I MAY KNOW HIM
Website Ministry of Michael F. Blume
www.mikeblume.com

Garden City Publications
Winnipeg, Manitoba

To

*Brandon, Ian,
Amber and Candice*

TABLE OF CONTENTS

Table of Contents iv
Author's Preface x

1 The Secret Garden 1
Crossing Jordan Is Not Dying And Going To Heaven 2
What's More Important: We Leave, Or Kingdom Come? 4
A Sword Stands At This Entrance 5
The Sword is a Good Thing 6
Our Canaan is the Rest 7
More Than Just Saying, "Lord, Lord" 9
The Labour is Mixing the Word With Faith 11
Undue Stress Upon Signs and Wonders 11
Mistaken Reliance Upon Sensational and Mystical Experiences 12

2 The Kingdom Foundation 15
Significance of the Sword 16
The Positive Purpose of the Sword 18
The Way to Enter is By The Lie-Slaying Sword 21

3 The Return of the King 25
Heaven On Earth 25
The King Dethroned 25
The Temple – Garden Pattern 26
Return Of The King 30
Ark Of The Covenant 35
Home To Stay 35
120 Priests In One Accord 37
Wasting the Christian Life 41
You Can Only Enjoy What You Know Is Yours 43

4 In the Presence of The One Who Dwells In The Holiest of Holies 44
  Entering the Lamb's Death 45
  Atonement Upon the Ark of the Covenant's Mercy Seat 46
  Nothing But the Blood 47
  Understanding How His Blood Alone is our Salvation 48
  The Church, the City on the Mountain 51
  The Church, The New Eve 53

5 A Place In The Holiest of Holies 55
  The Garden, the Temple & The New Jerusalem 56
  I Go to Prepare a Place For You 58
  The Way & the Place 59
  What Exactly Is This Place? 60
  We Will Make our Abode 64
  We Are the City 65

6 A Place For You At God's Throne 68
  Faith 70
  We Have the Real Temple 71
  Moses 72
  John 72
  God's Throne 73
  24 Elders 74
  Seven Lamps of Fire 75
  Sea of Glass and the Beasts 75
  The Tablets of Law and The Seven-Sealed Scroll ... 75
  Moses 75
  John 76
  The Revelation of What? 77

7 Barrier Of Knowledge, Pathway Of Love 79
  Living By One of Two Trees 80
  The Barrier 81
  "Forerunner" Implies We Follow 81
  What Is The Knowledge of Good and Evil? 83
  Not Knowledge in General 85

Judgmental Spirits 86
Backslider's Plight 87
Knowledge of Good and Evil Bars Us From God. 88
The Fundamental Need for Forgiveness 88
Law Lacks Grace 89
It Had To Be Grace 90
Ark Of The Covenant: Life Overrides
Knowledge 90
God Is A Forgiver 92
Love Doesn't Think the Worst 92

8 The Significance Of Zion And The Church. 95
Spirit Baptism Came Due To Christ's Right Hand
Enthronement 96
What is the Right Hand Throne All About? 99
David Takes Zion 100
Early Church Recognized that Zion Referred To
Them 102
An Example Of Applying Kingdom Truth To Our
Battles 104
Be Kingdom-Minded 105
Who Dares To Afflict The Kingdom People? 106

9 The Revelation of the Rock 108
"Hell" as the Grave 110
A Matter of Identities 112
If You Don't Taste Death Now, You Will Later . 113
You Might Know Jesus, But Does Jesus Know
You? 115
Self-Denial Awards Resurrection Power 117
Fruitless and False Prophets 117
The Father's Revelation Implies the Father's
Will 119
Stopping Works of Iniquity 120
The Rock, Iniquity and Knowing Jesus 121

10 The Kingdom is the Sheepfold 123
Jesus Knows His Sheep 125
Only Sheep Enter the Kingdom 126

The Call for the Sheep is Going Forth 127
The Will of the Father 128
The Spirit of Antichrist 130
Sheep and Wolves 131
The Cross Removes That Which the Devil Takes
Advantage Of 133
Are We Sure We Are Not Wolves? 134

11 The Kingdom Mountain of Zion **136**
Virgins 138
Follow Him 138
Firstfruits 138
A Pattern of Hearing One Thing, But Seeing
Another 139
The Church is Israel With Gentiles Added 140
The Rock of Zion – God's Kingdom 141
The Degree of Power Toward Us is Resurrection
Power 143

12 Mount Zion's Transfiguring Glory **148**
The Importance of Hearing About the Cross 149
Our Need to Deny Self 151
The Vital Need for "I Say Also Unto Thee" 153

13 Shining in Kingdom Glory **154**
A House is Only as Stable as its Foundation 155
Our House is Our Calling and Election 155
The Key to Being Known by Jesus 157
Shining in His Glory 158

14 Transfigured As Jesus Was Transfigured **161**
Virtue 162
Knowledge 162
Temperance 163
Patience 163
Godliness 163
Brotherly Kindness 163
Charity 163
Staring at Light Until We Shine 164

The Light of the Truth of the Cross Establishes Us.. 167
Thy Will Be Done, Not Ours 167

15 Three Men of the Mountains 169
Healing In The Wings of the Sun 170
Ministry of Light.. 171
Jacob Became Israel... 173
Turn, Turn, Turn... 174
Truth Must Change Our Way of Thinking 175
The Confession of the Rock.................................... 176

16 Back on the Kingdom Mountain In Eden 179
The Flaming Sword at the Garden Entrance......... 181
Living Sacrifices & the Will of the Father 182
Shining Once Again In the Garden Kingdom....... 183
Your Thinking First and Then Your Body............ 184
The Gates of Hell Shall Not Prevail....................... 186

17 It Is Enough: When the Sword Stops 187
Counting on the Flesh... 189

18 Measuring the Spirit River of Life 193
What are Leaves and Fruit?..................................... 195
The Law of the Spirit of Life................................... 196
Ceasing to Walk in Ungodly Counsel Because the River Touches our Ankles 197
Ankles, Knees & Loins: Members Presented to God to Use... 198
To Serve In Oldness of the Letter, or in Newness of the Spirit... 198
Ceasing to Stand in the Way of Sinners Because the River Touches our Knees................................. 200
Ceasing to Sit in the Seat of the Scornful Because the River Touches our Loins 201
Waters to Swim in 202
The River or the Wind – Trees or Chaff?.............. 202
In the River and the River in You 203

19 The Armour of God.................................. 204
    Glory Shining From The Face 206
    The Armour and God's Glory 208

20 Revelation of The Armour of Light 215
    Salvation by the Resurrection of Jesus 216
    "Arm" Yourself With This Understanding And
    Cease From Sin 216
    Get This Below Our Collar Bones and Into Our
    Hearts 217
    Likewise, We are Dead to Sin 218
    Living In Mortal Bodies, But Enjoying Victory
    Over Sin 220
    Let Not Sin Rule, But Let the Spirit Empower 221
    His Death Led to His Resurrection, And Our
    Resurrections! 222
    Put on the Armour By Putting on Christ 223
    Clothed With Armour of Light 224
    Arm Yourselves With the Same Mind 226

21 Vindication of the Priesthood 227
    More Almond Branches 228
    A Connecting Vision Involving the Candlesticks . 229
    The Tomb of Jesus Was In a Garden 234
    Kings, But Priests As Well 235
    Take a Bite of Eternal Life 236

Appendix   A Miracle of Confirmation! 237

AUTHOR'S PREFACE

This work of Volume II continues the overall concept of the restored Garden of Eden in the Kingdom of God today. The book has more of an emphasis upon the Kingdom power we now have in everyday situations of life. The idea of a restored Kingdom of God following the fall of mankind from the Garden Kingdom is a very important truth to understand in order for us to better fulfill the will of the Lord in our lives as believers. If we do not think the Kingdom is here for us today, we will obviously not expect to be able to enjoy Kingdom living. Everyone's conclusions in regards to the Kingdom are based upon our views of Eschatology. Improper understanding of Eschatology will lead to improper perception of our relationship in the Kingdom. I personally believe Jesus is presently at the *right hand position* on the throne of David in this Kingdom and has been there since His ascension (Mark 16:19). We have been born into this Kingdom by the water and Spirit (John 3:5). Just as it was originally in the Garden of Eden on earth, God has His present Kingdom operating in this world.

It has been alleged by some that the Kingdom of Heaven refers to something not yet experienced, waiting for us in "the great by and by." Some feel it is a distinct entity apart from the Kingdom of God. Scripture bears out that the Kingdom of God/Heaven is indeed something that is a present reality in this life.

The terms "Kingdom of God" and "Kingdom of Heaven" are synonymous. Notice how Jesus used them interchangeably.

> *Matthew 19:23-24   Then said Jesus unto his disciples, Verily I say unto you, That a rich man shall hardly* **enter into the kingdom of heaven.** *And again I say unto you, It is easier for a camel to go through the eye of a needle, than for a rich man to* **enter into the kingdom of God.**

Some claim the Kingdom of God is the work of God in the earth today, whereas the Kingdom of Heaven is something that will not take place until after the Lord comes. However, the Gospels indicate both Kingdoms were "at hand" when John the Baptist was still alive.

> *Matthew 4:12 Now when Jesus had heard that John was cast into prison, he departed into Galilee;...(17) From that time Jesus began to preach, and to say,* **Repent: for the kingdom of heaven is at hand.**

> *Mark 1:14-15 Now after that John was put in prison, Jesus came into Galilee, preaching the gospel of the kingdom of God, And saying, The time is fulfilled, and* **the kingdom of God is at hand: repent ye**, *and believe the gospel.*

I do not think this means the Kingdom of God was bound to occur whether the Jews rejected Jesus or not, while the Kingdom of Heaven was postponed because they rejected Him. It's just that Matthew's Gospel used the term "Kingdom of Heaven" while the other Gospels used "Kingdom of God" to describe the one and the same thing in identical parables and conversations that each Gospel recounts.

The Kingdom of God is here now. The King is on the throne, and we are born into this Kingdom. The Lord is restoring this *Kingdom revelation* to His people in these recent times, and people are awakening to their need to acknowledge it and act upon it.

Volume I related the overwhelming correlation of our present position in Christ with the intended purpose of Adam beyond the *cherubimic* and bladed barrier of the Garden entrance. Knowing we are indeed in a spiritually restored Edenic Kingdom, we can appreciate our purpose as being more than *twiddling our thumbs 'til Jesus comes*. We have a task set before us. God wants to manifest His Spirit and Kingdom power through you and I and thereby see His dominion manifested in this world. It is not the will of God to let the world go to pot, while we wait for an escape out of this place. In fact, Jesus prayed that we not be removed from the world but protected while in it in order to accomplish His purpose (John 17:15). This is in the same chapter where we read He gave us His glory as the Father had given Him glory (John 17:22). For what is this glory given to us? Did God not tell Adam to multiply, fill the earth, and have dominion? We are to fill the earth with Kingdom glory.

Let us seek more of this wonderful Kingdom truth, and learn how to play our parts in this world for His Kingdom's sake.

Michael F. Blume
May 2010

1

THE SECRET GARDEN

The entire Bible so wonderfully points all the way back to God's desired purpose for mankind in the Garden of Eden. The New Testament and the Church of Jesus Christ now has our Lord seated at the Right Hand throne. God has restored the Garden of Eden's Kingdom of God on earth. All believers are born again into this Kingdom (John 3:3, 5) with much to accomplish for the Lord long before He takes us away from this world.

We read of the Exodus story in the 3rd and 4th chapters of the book of Hebrews. There, we're told that Israel's opportunity to enter into the land of Canaan is compared to our goal as Christians today. Chapter 3 teaches that Israel manifested unbelief to enter Canaan at the time when God saw fit for them. This caused God to become angry. They missed the *entire purpose* of having been brought out of Egypt! Chapter 4 continues the thought and applies it to us today. There is a destination of *rest* for us in which God desires us to enter right now – so similar to Israel's goal of Canaan! These scriptures warn us that we must not provoke God to anger due to doubting Him for our successful entrance into this destination of *rest*. In other words, entering this rest stands as our purpose in some sense as entering Canaan was Israel's purpose in being freed from Egypt.

Since Israel was meant to set up its own Kingdom under God in that land, we can see that there is a *Kingdom Purpose* for us to enter in this life today! Could it be that many believers have provoked the Lord's anger as much as Israel did so long ago in not fulfilling this purpose? What exactly did these scriptures refer to when speaking of entering our *rest*?

CROSSING JORDAN IS NOT DYING AND GOING TO HEAVEN

Despite popular belief, crossing the Jordan into the Promised Land does not really speak of Heaven after this life is over. Israel fought and defeated giants in Canaan, while we read of no giants in the fields of Heaven that must be defeated. According to Hebrews chapters 3 and 4, Canaan represents a place of faith and power in God in this present life – in other words, our goal is Kingdom living. The thoughts of Hebrews 3:14 compare Israel's intended existence in Canaan to our opportunity to be partakers of Christ today. This partaking of Jesus Christ is this Kingdom Living. God had a purpose for Israel in the Promised Land. A kingdom of Israel would be established, God's laws would be fulfilled in that land, and in time Jesus Christ would come through their nation and be given to the world for its salvation. Just as Israel journeyed towards Canaan and then entered that country, Paul told us that we are to *come to all the fullness of Christ*, as though it were a journey's destination.

> *Ephesians 4:13* **Till we all come** *in the unity of the faith, and of the knowledge of the Son of God, unto a perfect man,* **unto** *the measure of the stature of* **the fulness of Christ***:*

I am reminded of the few words describing Jesus' preaching during the forty days after His resurrection.

> *Acts 1:3 To whom also he shewed himself alive after his passion by many infallible proofs, being seen of them forty days, and speaking of the things pertaining to the kingdom of God:*

For as many number of days as the spies of Israel searched out the Kingdom Land of Canaan, Jesus preached about the *Kingdom*. Israel had a preview of the land before they entered it. The same pattern is seen in the book of Acts. Jesus gave a 40-day preview before they entered the experience of the baptism of the Holy Spirit. The day of Pentecost was a crossing over into the Promised Land!

God gave us preaching and teaching ministries to bring us into all of the fullness of Christ (Eph. 4:11). Our *Canaan* is the fullness of Christ and we require Spirit baptism to appreciate it.

Paul also put it this way:

> *Ephesians 3:19 And to know the love of Christ, which passeth knowledge,* **that ye might be filled with all the fulness of God.**

Coming to the state of being wherein we experience the fullness of Christ is called *partaking of Christ* in scripture.

> *Hebrews 3:14 For we are made* **partakers of Christ***, if we hold the beginning of our confidence stedfast unto the end;*

The writing of Hebrews compared those who truly partake of Christ in all His fullness with Israel who were meant to enter the Promised Land in faith without doubting. This *Kingdom purpose* of the New Testament believer is meant to bring Christ forth from within our lives with His manifested presence, as much as Christ was to eventually come forth from the Promised Land of Canaan. Paul said Christ lived in him (Gal. 2:20). This enabled Paul to do great feats for the Kingdom of God by giving him the spiritual maturity of having become a partaker of Christ. Jesus actually lived through Paul in all the great accomplishments the apostle performed in the power of the Lord.

THE SECRET GARDEN

WHAT'S MORE IMPORTANT: WE LEAVE, OR KINGDOM COME?

The Kingdom of God is a very real Kingdom. Just because Jesus said it is not something you can see (Luke 17:20) does not mean it is not quite real and effective in this world. Many believers have misunderstood the Kingdom, and such confusion has led to the Dark Ages when the "church" attempted to conquer the world through what can only be called religious terrorism! Jesus, however, said the Kingdom is not something you can see, but is in you. It's a spiritual, invisible Kingdom.

In order for Paul to be used so mightily for the Kingdom's sake, he personally had to mature spiritually and come to the state of being a true partaker of Christ. Hebrews 3 taught that we are indeed such partakers of Christ *if we journey* towards it successfully by holding onto the confidence of our faith. We can be the people of Jesus Christ through whom He must manifest into the world around us (Hebrews 3:6). However, this is going to require more than a people who are *twiddling their thumbs 'til Jesus comes*. The Lord taught us to pray that His Kingdom would come and His will be done *in this world* as it is in Heaven. This means that while so many are waiting for the day when the Church will enter into the Kingdom in Heaven, Jesus told us to pray towards quite a different goal! The Kingdom must come down *here*, and His will be *done in this Earth now*.

It is of utmost importance that we recognize God's will to have His Kingdom operate in this world through our lives now. He placed the Garden in this world, not Heaven, and gave Adam dominion to rule in this world. What would make us think this mandate has changed? What would make us think that despite all the words of Jesus about the Kingdom of God, we are simply waiting and looking to die and go to Heaven or be raptured away at His coming, whichever comes first? I believe Jesus is indeed coming back again! However, that does not mean He does not want us to manifest His power in this Earth right now and see

His Kingdom in operation. He wants us to be used as mightily as the apostles were used in the earth.

A Sword Stands At This Entrance

> *Hebrews 4:9-12 There remaineth therefore a rest to the people of God. For he that is **entered into his rest**, he also hath ceased from his own works, as God did from his. Let us labour therefore to **enter into that rest**, lest any man fall after the same example of unbelief.* **For the word of God is quick, and powerful, and sharper than any twoedged sword**, *piercing even to the dividing asunder of soul and spirit, and of the joints and marrow, and is a discerner of the thoughts and intents of the heart.*

As a sword was placed at the entrance to the Garden of Eden (Gen. 3:24), a sword stands in the entrance of what the book of Hebrews called the *rest*. The writer said that there is a place of faith into which we must *enter*.

Again let me reiterate that the time for our entrance into this place is now. We can come boldly to the throne of grace right now (Heb. 4:16). It is supposed to be our goal as much as entering the Promised Land was the goal of the Hebrew people when they left Egypt. Note the many great parallels between the thought of entering our rest and Israel entering the Promised Land. The emphasis of the Lord's warning in the book of Hebrews is that Israel did not enter into their *Rest* due to unbelief. We are gravely warned...

> *Hebrews 4:11 Let us labour therefore to **enter** into that rest, lest any man fall after the same example of unbelief.*

Speaking of this entrance, we then read of the sword that is so reminiscent of the Garden entrance.

*Hebrews 4:12-13 For the word of God is quick, and powerful, and **sharper than any twoedged sword**, piercing even to the dividing asunder of soul and spirit, and of the joints and marrow, and is a discerner of the thoughts and intents of the heart. Neither is there any creature that is not manifest in his sight: but all are naked and opened unto the eyes of him with whom we have to do.*

After *saying* that we must ensure we *labour to enter this rest*, we read that we must do so "lest we fall after the same example of unbelief" as Israel. This occurred when Israel failed to enter Canaan. Their fear of the giants and well-walled cities held them back (Num. 13:28).

Hebrews 3:19 So we see that they could not enter in **because of unbelief.**

If we do not enter, it will be the result of unbelief in us as well.

Think of it. We must *labour to enter*, and we must *not disbelieve*. Put it altogether and realize we require *a labour of faith*. *Labour to believe*.

Notice what else is involved. We are encouraged to labour *because there is a sword* that is sharper than any other sword. Why would we want to labour for the reason of a sword being in the entrance? And what has that got to do with labouring *to believe?* Would not one rather *avoid to* enter, instead, due to that sword? Who wants to enter a door in which there is a sword whirling in every direction? It initially appears as though everyone is intended to *avoid* entering this doorway.

THE SWORD IS A GOOD THING

If we can catch the revelation, the sword actually stands as *an incentive* to enter. Who would have thought that there was a side to the concept of the sword at the Garden entrance that was positive? While the sword seems to stand as a discouragement to enter the Garden, Hebrews 4 informs us it is an *encouragement* for us to labour.

This sword accomplishes something we need. We read that it cuts directly into our souls and spirits, since it is the sword *of the Word of God*. In other words, God's Word is presented to a believer and it slices deep into our beings and is wielded by the Spirit *to seek out and destroy any unbelief that might be in our hearts*. That is a good thing! Unbelief is the element that hinders us from entering! Those who do not believe will simply not enter in, and we want to enter in! So, there we have a sword that is intended to remove this hindering element within all of us.

The way into the Garden is *the way of faith*. The sword goes to work to instil faith within our hearts, for faith comes by hearing, and hearing **by the Word** (Romans 10:17). Its cutting leaves us with the faith we need to enter because it destroys unbelief! Thank God for the Sword of His Word! It attacks and slays unbelief if we will only get that Word into our hearts and let it cut away!

The Gospel includes the information of *how we can believe* and not be barred out of the *rest* as Israel was barred out of the Promised Land. Now, if the Book of Hebrews was written to folks who were already saved and in the church, we must come to the realisation that the *Gospel message* does not end for us upon our initial experience of salvation! Not at all! The Gospel carries us all the way through this Christian journey into the place of completion in Christ and full maturity of the believer. It brings us into true Kingdom living. The Book of Hebrews proves to us that the Gospel must not only be believed upon in order to become a child of God, but that we must also reach the full extent of faith and power in Christ.

OUR CANAAN IS THE REST

Israel was *promised* to enter Canaan. Our *Promise* is to enter a spiritual place of Rest – the fullness of Christ.

THE SECRET GARDEN

> *Hebrews 4:1 Let us therefore fear, lest,* **a promise** *being left us of entering into his rest, any of you should seem to come short of it.*

How many of us know that true rest is a place of victory and no fear? It is a place of glory in Christ. It is a place where we enjoy all the promises that God has given to us instead of forever hoping we could get into such a place of confidence and surety. Otherwise, we will never enter due to unbelief, thinking that this destination is too good to be true.

Throughout the Gospel of the New Testament we read of the idea of entrance and proper faith that is required for it.

> *Luke 11:5-9 And he said unto them, Which of you shall have a friend, and shall go unto him at midnight, and say unto him, Friend, lend me three loaves; For a friend of mine in his journey is come to me, and I have nothing to set before him? And he from within shall answer and say, Trouble me not:* **the door is now shut**, *and my children are with me in bed; I cannot rise and give thee. I say unto you, Though he will not rise and give him, because he is his friend, yet because of his importunity he will rise and give him as many as he needeth. And I say unto you,* **Ask, and it shall be given you; seek, and ye shall find; knock, and it shall be opened unto you.**

In this illustration, the person *believes* that if he truly asks properly he will receive. As though a *door* blocks him from what he needs, he will see that door opened if the correct approach is made.

> *Luke 13:24-28* **Strive to enter** *in at the strait gate: for* **many,** *I say unto you,* **will seek to enter in, and shall not be able.** *When once the master of the house is risen up, and hath shut to the door, and ye begin to stand without, and to knock at the door, saying, Lord, Lord, open unto us; and*

> he shall answer and say unto you, I know you not whence ye are: Then shall ye begin to say, We have eaten and drunk in thy presence, and thou hast taught in our streets. But he shall say, I tell you, I know you not whence ye are; depart from me, all ye workers of iniquity. There shall be weeping and gnashing of teeth, when ye shall see Abraham, and Isaac, and Jacob, and all the prophets, in the kingdom of God, and you yourselves thrust out.

The door is actually the LORD, Himself (John 10:9).

The writer of Hebrews said there is a sword called the Word of God at the door. We know from the Bible that Jesus is also the Word of God, and the Word is God.

> John 1:1 In the beginning was the Word, and the Word was with God, and the Word was God.

> John 1:14 And the Word was made flesh, and dwelt among us, (and we beheld his glory, the glory as of the only begotten of the Father,) full of grace and truth.

There will be those who wish to enter through the door, but will not be able to because Jesus did not know them (see also Matt. 7:23). Though they ate and drank in His presence, and though He taught in their streets, He will say He did not know them. "Eating and drinking in his presence" speaks of hearing the word of God and feasting upon it. Jesus indicated that is not enough!

MORE THAN JUST SAYING, "LORD, LORD"

Simply going to Church and feasting on God's Word in His presence is not necessarily what causes Him to "know" us. This is the thought that the Book of Hebrews is trying to relate to us. We are instructed that we must *believe*.

Jesus is the door. We must face Him at the entrance.

THE SECRET GARDEN

John 10:1-2 Verily, verily, I say unto you, He that entereth not by the door into the sheepfold, but climbeth up some other way, the same is a thief and a robber. But he that entereth in by the door is the shepherd of the sheep.

John 10:7 Then said Jesus unto them again, Verily, verily, I say unto you, I am the door of the sheep.

I want to be a true sheep. So do you! I want to *enter* through this door! If we want to return to the Tree of Life to eat and live forever, and enter that rest, then we must pass this sword at the entrance. We must allow the sword to go to work and cut away any and all unbelief from our hearts. We cannot bypass the doorway! We can't go around the Word and the need to have faith planted within our hearts. Our Christianity must be based upon more than simply attending church services and hearing the Word. We must *do something* about what we hear. It must truly change our lives. We need to pass this grand test of Jesus, the Word, who is the door.

Jesus spoke about entrance in Matthew 7. He said we must *do something,* and not just talk about God, that we might enter.

Matthew 7:21-24 Not every one that saith unto me, Lord, Lord, shall enter into the kingdom of heaven; **but he that doeth the will of my Father** *which is in heaven. Many will say to me in that day, Lord, Lord, have we not prophesied in thy name? and in thy name have cast out devils? and in thy name done many wonderful works? And then will I profess unto them, I never knew you: depart from me, ye that work iniquity. Therefore* **whosoever heareth these sayings of mine, and doeth them***, I will liken him unto a wise man, which built his house upon a rock:*

We must *do the will of the Father.* We must hear Jesus' sayings and *do them.* Tying this truth with the information provided in

Hebrews 4, we learn that the *doing* Jesus spoke about involves *believing* – the labour to enter.

But what exactly is it that we must believe?

> *Hebrews 4:1-3 Let us therefore fear, lest, a promise being left us of entering into his rest, any of you should seem to come short of it. For unto us was the gospel preached, as well as unto them: but the word preached did not profit them, not being mixed with faith in them that heard it. For we which have believed do enter into rest, as he said, As I have sworn in my wrath, if they shall enter into my rest: although the works were finished from the foundation of the world.*

THE LABOUR IS MIXING THE WORD WITH FAITH

Notice that we discover what sort of labour we must exert in order to enter this rest. It is mixing the Word with Faith. Our hearts are our faculties that are able to both love and believe. To mix the Word with faith is to perform the labour of letting that Sword stick into our hearts. Believe the Word. Let the blade pierce your heart. When you choose to believe it, it will cut away unbelief and do a marvellous work of sheering away all the caking of unbelief inside us.

It is faith that takes us in, and not any amount of wonderful experiences or miracles we might perform. Some people think that a bolt of sensational power from God will forever set them free from doubt and unbelief. Not so.

UNDUE STRESS
UPON SIGNS AND WONDERS

Jesus said there will be *many* who make the mistake of thinking something else will serve as their ticket to the inside. He said that many will think that having performed miracles, having cast out devils, and many wonderful things accomplished in Jesus' name indicates whether or not we will enter. A false foundation for Christianity is thinking the operation of miracles and healings means we are what we need to be. "God would not be using me if I was not right in His eyes!" Not true! Jesus said people will not enter due to such a foundation. That foundation is like sand. Such people stress miracles, signs, and wonders more than anything else – a bad philosophy to live by.

"Go to this Church and you will see the miracles of the Bible."

Sensationalism really does appeal to the average person, and we need to have miracles, for there are needs that only a miracle from God can meet. But that is not what will get us into the Holiest. We must have the proper foundation if we wish to enter into this Kingdom of Heaven. Israel saw miraculous events in the wilderness before they came to Canaan and was refused to enter due to their fear and unbelief.

What is your idea of the basis of Christianity? If you were to explain to someone how to be saved and fulfil God's will, what would be your answer? If you were to help someone enter past the sword, what would you advise them?

MISTAKEN RELIANCE UPON SENSATIONAL AND MYSTICAL EXPERIENCES

Many think the success of their Christianity depends upon whether or not they can *feel the Spirit of God*. Let me say from the start that it is possible to sense the presence of God upon our lives. I have personally felt His presence many times. There is a need for it. But I have dealt with people who took this much too far. Some choose not to accept salvation unless they literally *feel something* when they hear the preaching of the Word while in Church. I've preached to many people about the proper *faith* they must exert in order to enter the threshold, and they understood every word I said. But it was all pushed to the side due to their false concept that they must *feel* something, or else they will not make that step. They believed that feeling God was some sort of indication from God that it is time for them to get saved.

I know a dear friend who sat in many Church meetings and heard the word of God again and again. He told me he was waiting *to feel something* before he made any effort to give his life for God. It seemed that his confidence in knowing that God wanted him to be saved was not based upon God's Word to that effect but upon whether or not God would give him the go-ahead through the means of letting him *feel His presence*. I told him that Jesus did not say, "he that feeleth God's Spirit shall be saved," but "he that believeth and is baptized shall be saved." (Mark 16:16). That is the reason Jesus said, "Teach all nations, baptizing them in the name" (Matt. 28:19). The Lord wants everyone to be saved. They simply need to know about it, and then it is their responsibility to act upon it! Paul taught the Romans that once a person knows of God's glory a choice must be made. Either glorify God as God by obeying the truth, or *hold the truth in unrighteousness* by disobeying it. Those who know truth and do nothing about it are fit only to receive God's wrath (Romans 1:18-21). We do not require a feeling in order to know for sure that God wants to save us. His will is that none perish. As soon as we know that, we need to comply!

I talked to another man who stood upon the verse that said, "No man cometh to me except the Father draw him." (John 6:44). He interpreted God's drawing as the *feeling of a mystical sensation* before He could properly believe, although he already knew the truth of what to believe. A thousand times NO! Once we simply *know the truth*, we have all that we need to make us free. The way the Father draws us to Jesus is by *informing us* of how to be saved. He gives us correct information about Jesus through a presentation of the Word in some form showing us what we must believe. We can know when God wants to save us by simply realizing that God let us learn the truth of how to be saved!

One minister was in an airport and overheard a woman behind him describe the same thing many Christians stress about their Christianity. He heard her say that *she felt* so much peace and love since she believed. She spoke of how everything was different for her since she believed. She told others how they must also believe so they can have this goal of all goals in their lives. He turned around expecting to see a Christian woman and found that she was a follower of Hare Krishna!

Any religion at all can provide you with a mystical experience of some kind of peace, but that is not what will take you through "the entrance." The false doctrine of the book of Mormon has an introduction page in it that tells you that you will *feel* a burning in the bosom to let you know the book is giving you the truth from God.

Jesus said we would *know the truth* and *the truth* would make us free (John 8:32). Our Christianity must be founded upon a proper foundation if we are going to enter God's rest, and it is not a foundation of *feelings*.

Christ's discussion with Peter gave us a key…

2

THE KINGDOM FOUNDATION

Matthew 16:15-18 He saith unto them, But whom say ye that I am? And Simon Peter answered and said, Thou art the Christ, the Son of the living God. And Jesus answered and said unto him, Blessed art thou, Simon Barjona: for flesh and blood hath not revealed it unto thee, but my Father which is in heaven. And I say also unto thee, That thou art Peter, and upon this rock I will build my church; and the gates of hell shall not prevail against it.

We must believe that Jesus is the Son of the Living God. He is exclusively worthy of praise. Jesus said *that* is the Rock upon which He will build His church. The foundation of the *Church* is the truth about *Jesus Christ*.

1 Corinthians 3:10-11 According to the grace of God which is given unto me, as a wise masterbuilder, I have laid the foundation, and another buildeth thereon. But let every man take heed how he buildeth thereupon. **For other foundation can no man lay than that is laid, which is Jesus Christ.**

We must have this foundation! There is none other!

2 Timothy 2:19 Nevertheless the foundation of God standeth sure, having this seal, The Lord knoweth them that are his. And, Let every one that nameth the name of Christ depart from iniquity.

THE KINGDOM FOUNDATION

Paul informed Timothy that there is more to standing on this foundation than simply knowing Who Jesus is. On the foundation of this Kingdom into which we must *enter* to be saved is a twofold inscription, as though it was a cornerstone engraved with information.

1. The Lord knoweth them that are his.
2. Let every one that nameth the name of Christ depart from iniquity.

Compare that with Jesus' words in Matthew:

1. I never knew you. (The Lord knoweth them that are his.)
2. Depart from me, ye workers of iniquity. (Let every one that nameth the name of Christ depart from iniquity.)

The Kingdom is represented by the New Jerusalem where Christ's throne sits. Look at its description.

> *Revelation 21:14* And the wall of the city had **twelve foundations**, and in them **the names of the twelve apostles** of the Lamb.

> *Ephesians 2:20* And are built upon **the foundation of the apostles** and prophets, Jesus Christ himself being the chief corner stone;

The foundation is the *truth* about Jesus. Forget about feelings or miracles. Simply obey the Bible.

SIGNIFICANCE OF THE SWORD

Genesis 3:24 not only tells us that a flaming sword stood at the entrance, but that this sword also *kept 'the way'* of the Tree of Life. To *keep* something means to *protect it* – to preserve it. God preserved 'the way' to the Tree of Life. He used a flaming sword to do it.

Notice He called it a *"way."* It is a pathway.

What was it that removed the woman from the Garden?

> *Genesis 3:1 Now the serpent was more subtil than any beast of the field which the LORD God had made. And he said unto the woman, Yea, hath God said, Ye shall not eat of every tree of the Garden?*

The serpent made the woman doubt *the Word of God*. Disbelief took mankind out and *disbelief continues to keep* people out today. We who *believe enter into that rest*.

God wants us to walk 'that way' of life and return to the Garden. He protected 'that way' from vanishing from existence. I think the devil would have loved to destroy 'that *way*' and see it removed from man's reach forever. He managed to get man to *doubt God's Word*, and get man kicked out of the Garden. But if he was able to destroy the actual *'way'* to the Tree of Life, he would surely have done it. However, it was as though God said, "You can lie, devil, and I will leave man to decide whether or not to believe you, or to believe my Word. I will not *make man* do anything. But you will not destroy 'the *way'* of the Tree of Life. I will *keep* it for man to one day enter back in again should he choose to believe me in the future."

> *Matthew 7:14 Because strait is the gate, and narrow is* **the way, which leadeth unto life**, *and few there be that find it.*

So God *kept the way with a flaming sword.* This sword was flaming. It was alive.

> *Ephesians 6:17 ...and the sword of the Spirit, which is the word of God:*

The *sword* is a picture of the Word of God. Hebrews 4:12 says, the Word of God is quick (*alive*), powerful, and sharper than any two-edged sword. This is stated in the Book of Hebrews. Hebrews stated our need to resist falling after the same example of unbelief that Israel manifested. Israel did this when they failed to enter Canaan. We can, therefore, see that unbelief both put man out and keeps man out. This means that the sword is still there!

THE POSITIVE PURPOSE OF THE SWORD

God preserved 'the way' to that Tree of Life because He desired to have us walk it and return once again but without sin. Recall that the Lord thrust man out of the Garden lest he eat of the fruit of life and live forever with sin still in him. He put that sword there to ensure 'that way' remains available. Perhaps God would have removed the Tree of Life if man had been irrecoverable from his sin, but thanks be to God that the Tree is still intended for mankind. That same sword of the Word will go to work if people will only think to take 'that way' – that pathway of faith and Truth – and walk there.

You say, "It's a sword, though! It will slay me."

No! The sword is the Word of God. There is only one thing the Word of God slays, and that is a lie. In this way it keeps out anyone who believes a lie (Rev. 21:27). The sword will remove the lie, or else we cannot enter.

If you want to enter into the place God created for you, then you must let the Word work. Let it cut away! This precious Word will cut away all unbelief from your heart! It removes doubt. Unbelief causes us to fear. Only those who take a step of faith into '*that way*' will let the Word work away at their hearts.

Too many say, "I am not going to go *that* way! There are many ways to come to God."

There is only one way.

> *John 10:1-7 Verily, verily, I say unto you, He that entereth not by the door into the sheepfold, but climbeth up some other way, the same is a thief and a robber. But he that entereth in by the door is the shepherd of the sheep. To him the porter openeth; and the sheep hear his voice: and he calleth his own sheep by name, and leadeth them out. And when he putteth forth his own sheep, he goeth before them, and the sheep follow him: for they know his voice. And a stranger will they not follow, but will flee from him: for they know not the voice of strangers. This parable spake Jesus unto them: but they understood not what things they were which he spake unto them. Then said Jesus unto them again, Verily, verily, I say unto you, I am the door of the sheep.*

Jesus even referred to the need for us to *enter* a certain place in which He wants us to be in these words above.

He is the door to the sheepfold. It's a place into which He wants us to enter. Furthermore, He said that if we try to go in *any other way*, we are *robbers*. If we try to go in another way besides *the door of the sheepfold*, we are entering illegally. *There is only one way to enter into this place.*

> *Acts 4:10-12 Be it known unto you all, and to all the people of Israel, that by the name of Jesus Christ of Nazareth, whom ye crucified, whom God raised from the dead, even by him doth this man stand here before you whole. This is the stone which was set at nought of you builders, which is become the head of the corner. Neither is there salvation in any other: for there is none other name under heaven given among men, whereby we must be saved.*

Those were bold statements to make, and the hearers thought so, too.

> *Acts 4:13-14 Now* **when they saw the boldness of Peter and John**, *and perceived that they were unlearned*

and ignorant men, they marveled; and they took knowledge of them, that they had been with Jesus. And beholding the man which was healed standing with them, they could say nothing against it.

People saw a genuine work of God. Coupled with that work came a saying they didn't necessarily want to hear. However, the Name that was responsible for the miracle of Peter and John *is also the only name that will save you.* No other name and no other religious idea aside from the cross of Jesus Christ will save a soul. The antagonists were stunned because they had to admit the miracle was genuine!

No other name is ever going to be given under heaven by which we can be saved *other than Jesus Christ.*

*John 14:6 Jesus saith unto him, I am **the way**, the truth, and the life: no man cometh unto the Father, but by me.*

1Pet 3:18 For Christ also hath once suffered for sins, the just for the unjust, that he might bring us to God, being put to death in the flesh, but quickened by the Spirit:

Jesus brought us to God by the only way possible. *He* suffered *for sins.* The only way to deal with our sins is *to die with Jesus.*

We read of the *way* to enter the Garden. It is protected by a flaming Sword. Jesus said "I am the way." We also learn that the means for Christ to be *the way* to get us to God was through His suffering as us.

God made Adam king when He put him into the Garden. He said, "Adam, have dominion over the earth." However, Adam was later *dethroned.* So, there is the idea of *a throne* in that directive from God in the place where you can be seated with Christ and rule again. But satan is going to cloud that understanding from your mind if he can.

God told Israel they would rule their own land as opposed to being slaves in Egypt. What a change after being slaves for over four hundred years! When time came to enter the land of Canaan and rule, they *doubted* and were *afraid to enter*.

Unbelief causes people to *fear*. If we do not *believe* we can conquer our enemy then we will *fear* our enemy. When unbelief is dealt with, and the Word cuts away the doubt and corrects our thinking, giving us faith, we will no longer fear but will be *emboldened*.

After we read of a sword and an entrance in the book of Hebrews, we then read the following:

> *Hebrews 4:16 Let us therefore come boldly unto the throne of grace, that we may obtain mercy, and find grace to help in time of need.*

Look at the sequence of thought in Hebrews 4.

1. ENTER REST
2. DO NOT DISBELIEVE
3. A SWORD OF TRUTH IS THERE AT THE ENTRANCE to cut away your unbelief.
4. THEN COME BOLDLY (ENTER) TO THE THRONE.

Boldness is the result of *faith* that causes *fear* to be removed. We are no longer afraid and suddenly we have what it takes to *enter in* – boldness.

THE WAY TO ENTER IS BY THE LIE-SLAYING SWORD

'The *way*' is kept by the flaming sword. So if you want to find 'the way', go to the sword.

It only stands to reason that there indeed is a throne in that place of rest. Adam was king in there, and we are told that we can find *mercy* at that *throne*. What was it that stood inside a very holy place that was like a throne and corresponded to *mercy*? There was the Mercy Seat atop the Ark of the Covenant in that

THE KINGDOM FOUNDATION

secret place called the Holiest of Holies. The *veil* barred this most holy place.

The veil had cherubim on it just as cherubim were at the Garden entrance. The veil was rent in two when Jesus died. So a sword is indeed involved!

The veil speaks of Jesus' flesh (Heb. 10:20). When that veil ripped, the cherubim ripped with it. That is symbolic of how we died *with* Him. You must enter through that path.

So the unbelief that the *sword* is trying to remove from you is the unbelief that says Jesus did not have to die on the cross for you to go to Heaven. Every false religion and false form of Christianity skirts around the death of Christ on the cross as our way to glory.

Notice that many incidents from the Bible speak of the same message of death at the entrance.

- The blood of a lamb was splattered on the entrance in the Hebrew homes in Egypt, saving them from death.
- The veil barrier covering the Holiest of Holies ripped when Jesus died.
- The sword of the Word of God stands in the entrance into rest.

> *Acts 16:31 And they said,* **Believe** *on the Lord Jesus Christ, and thou shalt be saved, and thy house.*

Since our enemy cannot remove the sword nor remove *the way*, he attacks *you and your mind*. The only way you are going to enter this secret place is to pass through the sword and let the Word make a believer out of you.

God just plainly put it this way: Believe my word or perish.

> *Ephesians 2:5-8 Even when we were dead in sins, hath quickened us together with Christ, (by grace ye are saved;) And hath raised us up together, and made us sit together in heavenly places in Christ Jesus: That in the ages to come he*

might shew the exceeding riches of his grace in his kindness toward us through Christ Jesus. For by grace are ye saved through faith; and that not of yourselves: it is the gift of God:

Psalm 91:1-10 **He that dwelleth in the secret place** *of the most High shall abide under the shadow of the Almighty. I will say of the LORD, He is my refuge and my fortress: my God; in him will I trust. Surely he shall deliver thee from the snare of the fowler, and from the noisome pestilence. He shall cover thee with his feathers, and under his wings shalt thou trust: his truth shall be thy shield and buckler. Thou shalt not be afraid for the terror by night; nor for the arrow that flieth by day; Nor for the pestilence that walketh in darkness; nor for the destruction that wasteth at noonday. A thousand shall fall at thy side, and ten thousand at thy right hand; but it shall not come nigh thee. Only with thine eyes shalt thou behold and see the reward of the wicked. Because thou hast made the LORD, which is my refuge, even the most High, thy habitation; There shall no evil befall thee, neither shall any plague come nigh thy dwelling.*

This place is secret because it is hidden away from man by the veiling. It is *the Secret Garden*.

Did you catch what the Psalm said? Verse 2 noted that the one who dwells there is one who made a decision and said, "I will say of the Lord, He is my refuge and my fortress. My God. In Him will I trust." Think of that word "trust". The people who made a decision to believe this Bible are the people who dwell in this *secret place*. How did they get in there? They trusted.

How could they trust? They made a decision to take God's Word for what it says and accept Jesus as the door of the sheepfold, and trust in Him and nobody else. And guess what? They discovered that the Bible was correct! They are now inside!

Until we believe that *Jesus*, and Him crucified, is the *'only way'*, we will remain outside.

THE KINGDOM FOUNDATION

Galatians 1:8-9 But though we, or an angel from heaven, preach any other gospel unto you than that which we have preached unto you, let him be accursed. As we said before, so say I now again, If any man preach any other gospel unto you than that ye have received, let him be accursed.

What is the Gospel? 1 Cor. 15:1-4 reveals the Gospel to be the teachings of the death, burial and resurrection of Jesus Christ.

God turned the *Hebrews' homes* into places of *refuge* from death in Egypt *by one thing and one thing alone*. The Blood of a lamb was put on the doorways!

Church, Jesus is the door. He is the Lamb slain. He said we must enter into this goal of the born-again believer into fullness of maturity and activity in the Kingdom of God by Him alone.

3

THE RETURN OF THE KING

Let's look more closely at the thought of the Garden as represented by the Tabernacle and the Temple of God.

> *Genesis 2:8 And the LORD God planted a Garden eastward in Eden; and there he put the man whom he had formed.*

HEAVEN ON EARTH

God placed a man in the Garden in Eden and He intended that Paradise to be the home of mankind. The name "Eden" literally means Paradise, or *Heaven*. Man was actually given a Heaven on earth, but he was driven out from this Paradise due to sin. In disobedience to God, Adam partook of the fruit from the Tree of the Knowledge of Good and Evil. God preserved the possibility of recovering man from sin by banning him from the Garden of Eden but preserving the Garden where man could eat the fruit of life and live forever at a later date.

THE KING DETHRONED

Adam lost his home.

THE RETURN OF THE KING

A king lost his throne that day – banished from his own throne room. I say that Adam was *a king* because God gave *dominion* to him when He created him. Since we know that Kings were "anointed" by God during Old Testament times, we understand that Adam must have similarly been "anointed" to rule. When a man became king, he was anointed with oil indicating God's Spirit resting upon him to strengthen him to rule. When Samuel anointed David, the Bible tells us that *the Spirit of the Lord came upon him*. So, the oil of anointing represented the Spirit of God empowering a person's life. As oil oozes, flowing over the skin to soothe and comfort, and is absorbed into one's flesh, the Spirit of God comforts us and is like spiritual "ointment." In fact, the term *anointing* comes from the term *ointment*. The thought of ointment is to be considered when thinking of the Spirit.

Jesus said the Spirit *anointed* him (Luke 4:18) in fulfillment of Isaiah 61:1.

Adam lost his anointing.

THE TEMPLE – GARDEN PATTERN

Throughout the construct of the Temple of God, we read of shadows and memories of the Garden of Eden in the book of 2 Chronicles.

> *2 Chronicles 3:7 He overlaid also the house, the beams, the posts, and the walls thereof, and the doors thereof, with gold; and graved cherubims on the walls.*

> *2 Chronicles 3:10 And in the most holy house he made two cherubims of image work, and overlaid them with gold.*

> *2 Chronicles 3:14 And he made the vail of blue, and purple, and crimson, and fine linen, and wrought cherubims thereon.*

There were other "Garden" elements mentioned in the Temple of God, also.

2 Chronicles 3:16 And he made chains, as in the oracle, and put them on the heads of the pillars; and made an hundred pomegranates, and put them on the chains.

2 Chronicles 4:13 And four hundred pomegranates on the two wreaths; two rows of pomegranates on each wreath, to cover the two pommels of the chapiters which were upon the pillars.

With pillars like trees and pomegranates, the picture was definitely "Garden-like." Even the candlesticks were shaped like trees.

Exodus 25:31-35 And thou shalt make a candlestick of pure gold: of beaten work shall the candlestick be made: his shaft, and his branches, his bowls, his knops, and his flowers, shall be of the same. And six branches shall come out of the sides of it; three branches of the candlestick out of the one side, and three branches of the candlestick out of the other side: Three bowls made like unto almonds, with a knop and a flower in one branch; and three bowls made like almonds in the other branch, with a knop and a flower: so in the six branches that come out of the candlestick. And in the candlestick shall be four bowls made like unto almonds, with their knops and their flowers. And there shall be a knop under two branches of the same, and a knop under two branches of the same, and a knop under two branches of the same, according to the six branches that proceed out of the candlestick.

Why was this entire Garden theme in the Temple? God's mind was primarily upon the Garden of Eden from which man was driven because of his sin. He still desired man to return long after Adam was cast out when God directed Moses to build the Tabernacle and Solomon to build the Temple. It was still His will to have a King in Eden, as it were, ruling over the world.

The Temple was a picture of the Garden of Eden. We already noted how a veil was erected across the entrance into the "oracle" or the inner sanctum of the Temple. This Oracle, also called the Most Holy Place, was where the Ark of the Covenant was positioned in the Temple. Over the Ark, upon its Mercy Seat, was where God's presence manifested (Ex. 25:22).

Upon this veil was the embroidered work of the cherubim that were first mentioned to be guardians of Eden's eastern entrance, keeping or protecting the way of the Tree of Life (Ex. 26:31). It is no coincidence that the entrance to the Most Holy Place in the Temple was on the east of that particular room. So, we find that a person who intended on entering the most holy place would confront a barrier of a veil with the likeness of cherubim sewn into it, just as Adam would have confronted cherubim had he attempted to enter the Garden after his expulsion.

Indeed, the Temple portrayed the Garden of Eden, with the very account of Adam's fall in view, due to the presence of a barrier of cherubim.

Consider these points. Man should have ruled the world from the Garden under God. The Temple is a portrait of the Garden in model form. We must then conclude that the Temple involved the thought of a man returning to the Most Holy Place, the counterpart of the Garden, and ruling also. *This is precisely what we find!*

Cherubim symbolize mankind and his authority with God. They refer to the anointed human being, given rule to dominate the world and subdue it. This was no indication for man to dominate man, but rather for man to dominate the planet.

Remember we discussed the issue of the faces of the cherubim representing the four kingdoms of creatures Adam specifically named during his time in the Garden (Gen. 2:20; 3:20). Noah's covenant involved the mention of the cattle, beasts, fowl and man, too (Gen. 9:10). The fact that Noah's covenant made mention of these creatures, stresses to us the message that God had Adam's presence in the Garden in mind in Noah's day. The presence of Cherubim throughout the Temple likewise shows this picture of man's dominion and anointing to rule the world. The Temple was filled with the images of Cherubim – emblems of man's authority in the Garden.

The particular layout of the Temple is reminiscent of the Garden. We should pay close attention to the goings on in the Temple, for surely God would have a message therein concerning man's return to the Garden of Eden.

Ezekiel's vision of the Temple of God highlighted the eastern entrance to the Temple. We read that God's glory came from the east and his voice was like the sound of many waters (Ezek. 1:24). The earth shined with His glory (Ezek. 43:2). Recall that Paul referred to man as "the glory of God" (1 Cor. 11:7). This perfectly fits the scenario that Ezekiel claims he saw in the vision. We read that the glory that Ezekiel saw was, "...according to the appearance of the vision which I saw, even according to the vision that I saw when I came to destroy the city: and the visions were like the vision that I saw by the river Chebar; and I fell upon my face" (Ezek. 43:3; Comp. Ezek. 1:1).

Ezekiel wrote of the four living creatures he saw there as mentioned earlier – the cherubim. So we find that the "glory" he saw came from the east, as described in Chapter 43, and involved Cherubim. Here we have a Temple and the idea of Cherubim is noted alongside the Temple! In other words, we are reading about something to do with Adam and the Garden of Eden again as we read Ezekiel chapter 43.

The glory of Ezekiel 43, described in chapter 1, also involved more descriptions of the Cherubim. Among the many more descriptions of the Cherubim, we also find explanation of the "chariot" in which the Cherubim were carried. Wheels were mentioned. There was a wheel within a wheel. Eyes were said to be all over the wheels. There was *a firmament* over the heads of the four Cherubim. The firmament appeared to be like crystal.

THE RETURN OF THE KING

A *firmament* is an expanse, or base upon which something rests. It is a solid extended surface. A voice was heard over the heads of the Cherubim, and a throne was positioned on the solid surface.

> *Ezekiel 1:26-28 And above the firmament that was over their heads was the likeness of a throne, as the appearance of a sapphire stone: and upon the likeness of the throne was the likeness as the appearance of a man above upon it. And I saw as the colour of amber, as the appearance of fire round about within it, from the appearance of his loins even upward, and from the appearance of his loins even downward, I saw as it were the appearance of fire, and it had brightness round about. As the appearance of the bow that is in the cloud in the day of rain, so was the appearance of the brightness round about.* **This was the appearance of the likeness of the glory of the LORD.** *And when I saw it, I fell upon my face, and I heard a voice of one that spake.*

RETURN OF THE KING

A man sat upon the throne! This is precisely the picture of Adam ruling in the Garden! A man was seen sitting on a throne over the heads of the Cherubim. All of this was the glory that Ezekiel saw as he stood by the *eastern* entrance to the Temple in chapter 43.

So far we saw Cherubim all over the Temple – the emblems of man's anointing and dominion while in the Garden of Eden. We saw the Garden layout with a most holy place reminiscent of the Garden, barred by Cherubim on a veil. Now we understand that the Glory Ezekiel saw coming from the east towards this Temple involves Cherubim again, and a throne with a man seated over the heads of those Cherubim.

This picture of a King seated on a throne above the heads of others, and moving, is a familiar picture. Kings of old were carried in *caravan style* on *a throne held aloft by servants using rods to carry the throne over their heads.* What we see is a King carried on his throne by servants as we read Ezekiel's description of the glory of God! And all of this surrounds the Temple that portrays the Garden from whence a King, Adam, lost his dominion. Man was created to be God's image and the glory of God! It all fits perfectly!

What happens with this Glory of God, this human King held aloft on a throne?

> *Ezekiel 43:4 And the glory of the LORD came into the house by the way of the gate* **whose prospect is toward the east**.

Ezekiel saw the glory of God, a human King on a throne accompanied by Cherubim, enter the Temple in the *eastern* entrance. Was this not reminiscent of the expulsion of Adam from the *eastern* entrance to the throne room of the Garden?

> *Genesis 3:24 So he drove out the man; and he placed at the* **east of the Garden** *of Eden Cherubims, and a flaming sword which turned every way, to keep the way of the Tree of Life.*

We are seeing a King return to the Garden in symbolic fashion when we see the Glory of God enter the Temple through the eastern gate.

Who is this King? Who is this man?

Back in Chapter 1 of Ezekiel, take note of all there is to read of the appearance of the man who sat on the throne.

> *Ezekiel 1:27-28 And I saw as the colour of amber, as the appearance of fire round about within it, from the appearance of his loins even upward, and from the appearance of his loins even downward, I saw as it were the appearance of fire, and it had brightness round about. As the appearance of the bow that is in the cloud in the day of rain, so was the appearance of*

THE RETURN OF THE KING

> *the brightness round about. This was the appearance of the likeness of the glory of the* LORD. *And when I saw it, I fell upon my face, and I heard a voice of one that spake.*

From his loins upward the man was the colour of amber. From the loins downward he was the colour of fire. A rainbow was around His head.

John saw a similar picture of Jesus in the vision he received while at Patmos.

> *Revelation 1:13-15 And in the midst of the seven candlesticks one like unto the Son of man, clothed with a garment down to the foot, and girt about the paps with a golden girdle. His head and his hairs were white like wool, as white as snow; and his eyes were as a flame of fire; his feet like unto fine brass, as if they burned in a furnace; and his voice as the sound of many waters.*

> *Revelation 1:17-18 And when I saw him, I fell at his feet as dead. And he laid his right hand upon me, saying unto me, Fear not; I am the first and the last: I am he that liveth, and was dead; and, behold, I am alive for evermore, Amen; and have the keys of hell and of death.*

John saw Jesus Christ in the same likeness that Ezekiel saw a man sitting on a throne, called the glory of God!

The *amber* colour of the man from his loins upward was *the golden girdle* John saw on Jesus Christ. The *fires* from the loins downward were *the legs like brass burning in a furnace.*

Ezekiel saw a man indeed! He saw Jesus Christ in a vision from the perspective of Ezekiel's future. The earth shined with his Glory in Ezekiel 43:2.

John saw Him amidst seven golden candlesticks – the same candlesticks that were seen in the Temple! Over and again we are seeing throughout the Word of God pictures that portray the scene of the Garden of Eden from whence King Adam was cast.

But instead of seeing Adam return, we see another man, Jesus Christ, enter the Sanctuary to rule.

God's throne is shown to John with a rainbow around it as Ezekiel saw a rainbow around the throne on the firmament.

> *Revelation 4:2-3   And immediately I was in the spirit: and, behold, a throne was set in heaven, and one sat on the throne. And he that sat was to look upon like a jasper and a sardine stone:* **and there was a rainbow round about the throne***, in sight like unto an emerald.*

Contrasted to Adam, Jesus Christ is called the Last Adam.

> *1Corinthians 15:45   And so it is written, The first man Adam was made a living soul; the last Adam was made a quickening spirit.*

When would this return to Eden's Garden occur? When would this vision of Ezekiel be fulfilled? When would the King of Kings be transported on a throne of glory into the Temple of God's Paradise on Earth?

To find the answer, notice what the glory of God, this human King, said.

> *Ezekiel 43:5-12   So the spirit took me up, and brought me into the inner court; and, behold, the glory of the LORD filled the house. And I heard him speaking unto me out of the house; and the man stood by me. And he said unto me,* **Son of man, the place of my throne, and the place of the soles of my feet, where I will dwell in the midst of the children of Israel for ever, and my holy name, shall the house of Israel no more defile,** *neither they, nor their kings, by their whoredom, nor by the carcases of their kings in their high places. In their setting of their threshold by my thresholds, and their post by my posts, and the wall between me and them, they have even*

> *defiled my holy name by their abominations that they have committed: wherefore I have consumed them in mine anger. Now let them put away their whoredom, and the carcases of their kings, far from me,* **and I will dwell in the midst of them for ever.** *Thou son of man, shew the house to the house of Israel, that they may be ashamed of their iniquities: and let them measure the pattern. And if they be ashamed of all that they have done, shew them the form of the house, and the fashion thereof, and the goings out thereof, and the comings in thereof, and all the forms thereof, and all the ordinances thereof, and all the forms thereof, and all the laws thereof: and write it in their sight, that they may keep the whole form thereof, and all the ordinances thereof, and do them. This is the law of the house; Upon the top of the mountain the whole limit thereof round about shall be most holy. Behold, this is the law of the house.*

Israel represents the people of God in the Church today. The Church is called "the Israel of God" in Galatians 6:16. "Israel" actually means "Prince with God." It describes Adam in his ordained status as King under God. The actual nation of Israel in Old Testament times foreshadowed humanity and the spiritual Kingdom of God made of people from all nations today, saved by the blood of Jesus Christ, as Israel was saved from Egypt.

Israel speaks of a restored humanity back in the Kingdom with a man who is King. Jesus Christ is 100% God and is 100% human. Adam was thrust from the Garden due to sin. Since a man brought death, it was a principle that a man, Jesus Christ, was also required to bring resurrection from the dead (1 Cor. 15:21).

Since one man, Adam, could cause many to become sinners by his single act, the principle holds that another sinless man could render many to be righteous by His single act (Rom. 5:19). But the status of that one man would have to be like that which Adam held. For this reason Christ was supernaturally brought into the world without sin, as Adam was made. The only difference was that Adam's parents were God and the earth. Jesus Christ is the Lord from Heaven (1 Cor. 15:47).

The only way man could bring resurrection from the dead was for one of us to be sinless. God could not send an angel to die for our sins. An angel cannot identify with us and, therefore, die as us. Simply put, we are not angels. The only possible way for a man to exist without sin was for God Himself to become manifest in flesh as a man (1 Tim. 3:16). Such a man could die in our places and thus identify with us.

But when would this entrance of man back into the Garden be fulfilled?

ARK OF THE COVENANT

Another note we must look at is the Ark of the Covenant that was placed inside the most holy place. The Ark was a chest with a Mercy Seat upon it, held aloft when transported by people holding staves (Exodus 25:10-22). This is precisely the same picture we saw in the Glory of God in Ezekiel's vision. A man sat on *a throne held over the heads of the Cherubim*. The Ark of the Covenant is a picture of a King's throne to be transported by servants *holding it over their heads* in honour of the King. Take notice that Cherubim were on the Mercy Seat!

HOME TO STAY

So long as the Ark was transported with staves, we know that the King was not permanently situated inside the throne room. With that in mind, read in Ezekiel's vision how the glory of God was transported from the east into the Temple's east gate. Then His glory filled the Temple.

The literal Temple of Israel experienced this same picture centuries before Ezekiel saw the vision.

THE RETURN OF THE KING

> *2 Chronicles 5:1 Thus all the work that Solomon made for the house of the LORD was finished: and Solomon brought in all the things that David his father had dedicated; and the silver, and the gold, and all the instruments, put he among the treasures of the house of God.*

Solomon built the Temple of God. Upon its completion, all the leaders of Israel were summoned to its dedication. The Ark of the Covenant was fetched.

> *2 Chronicles 5:2 Then Solomon assembled the elders of Israel, and all the heads of the tribes, the chief of the fathers of the children of Israel, unto Jerusalem, to bring up the Ark of the covenant of the LORD out of the city of David, which is Zion.*

> *2 Chronicles 5:5 And they brought up the Ark, and the Tabernacle of the congregation, and all the holy vessels that were in the Tabernacle, these did the priests and the Levites bring up.*

The bringing of the Ark involved a particular fashion of transport. We noted that staves were inserted in rings upon the Ark that it might be carried using these rods. David learned the hard way that the Ark must only be transported using men carrying it with staves, after having seen Uzzah's death when they carried the ark by ox cart to Jerusalem.

> *1 Chronicles 15:13-15 For because ye did it not at the first, the LORD our God made a breach upon us, for that we sought him not after the due order. So the priests and the Levites sanctified themselves to bring up the Ark of the LORD God of Israel. And the children of the Levites bare the Ark of God upon their shoulders with the staves thereon, as Moses commanded according to the word of the LORD.*

I wondered what the significance of carrying the Ark with staves was until I studied these thoughts. The Ark represented God's glory and Kingship being transported as though on a throne held aloft over the heads of the King's servants! *Imagine the degradation of a King riding in His throne on an ox cart!*

> *2 Chronicles 5:7-9 And the priests brought in the Ark of the covenant of the LORD unto his place, to the oracle of the house, into the most holy place, even under the wings of the cherubims: For the cherubims spread forth their wings over the place of the Ark, and the cherubims covered the Ark and the staves thereof above. And they drew out the staves of the Ark, that the ends of the staves were seen from the Ark before the oracle; but they were not seen without. And there it is unto this day.*

They brought the Ark into the most holy place, the very room that identified with the Garden of Eden, whose veil of Cherubim barred people out! Then they removed the staves. The Ark had been constructed in Moses' day, and from that day until this day of Temple dedication, the staves remained in the Ark to be used to carry it. But finally the staves were removed to indicate that the King was then there to stay!

When would this foreshadow be fulfilled?

120 PRIESTS IN ONE ACCORD

> *2 Chronicles 5:11-14 And it came to pass, when the priests were come out of the holy place: (for all the priests that were present were sanctified, and did not then wait by course: Also the Levites which were the singers, all of them of Asaph, of Heman, of Jeduthun, with their sons and their brethren, being arrayed in white linen, having cymbals and psalteries and harps, stood at the east end of the altar, and with them an hundred and twenty priests sounding with trumpets:) It came even to pass, as the trumpeters and singers were as one, to*

THE RETURN OF THE KING

> *make one sound to be heard in praising and thanking the LORD; and when they lifted up their voice with the trumpets and cymbals and instruments of musick, and praised the LORD, saying, For he is good; for his mercy endureth for ever: that then the house was filled with a cloud, even the house of the LORD; So that the priests could not stand to minister by reason of the cloud: for the glory of the LORD had filled the house of God.*

After the Ark was placed in the Most Holy Place, 120 priests blew trumpets and singers began to sing. When they finally sounded forth as one single voice, in one accord, suddenly the Temple was filled with God's glory and the priests fell on their faces. They could not stand and minister any longer.

This parallels the vision Ezekiel saw in Chapter 43 of his prophecies. He saw the glory of God enter the east gate of the Temple, as the Ark was carried through the east gate into the Most Holy Place. God's glory filled both the Temple of Solomon and Ezekiel's Temple.

Hebrews 9 reads that the Tabernacle is a grand display foreshadowing the work of Christ and the New Testament. Obviously the Temple was likewise a foreshadow of Christ's work.

Recall the King's words in Ezekiel's vision:

> *Ezekiel 43:7 And he said unto me, Son of man, the place of my throne, and the place of the soles of my feet, where I will dwell in the midst of the children of Israel for ever, and my holy name, shall the house of Israel no more defile, neither they, nor their kings, by their whoredom, nor by the carcases of their kings in their high places.*

Notice the element of the place of His throne where He would dwell forever. The inauguration of the Temple in 2 Chronicles 5 and the vision of Ezekiel in chapter 43 are foreshadows of the same event that was yet to come. The idea of removing staves to no more transport the Ark in 2 Chronicles, and the mention of the King dwelling there forever, both point to a time when Christ would enter the Garden/Sanctuary to permanently sit as King of Kings over the earth.

The King has returned, and man must remain clean and not repeat Adam's sin again. This is entirely a reference to man's overall return to the Garden of Eden in symbolic fashion.

When would this be fulfilled? The clues are provided for us. 120 priests blew trumpets and the glory filled the house. This very thing occurred already!

> *Acts 1:15 And in those days Peter stood up in the midst of the disciples, and said, (the number of names together were about* **an hundred and twenty,***)*

120 people entered an upper room as directed by Jesus Christ just before Jesus left the world. He told them to wait there to receive the Holy Ghost baptism of power.

> *Acts 1:4-5 And, being assembled together with them, commanded them that they should not depart from Jerusalem, but wait for the promise of the Father, which, saith he, ye have heard of me. For John truly baptized with water; but ye shall be baptized with the Holy Ghost not many days hence.*

A particular day arrived that happened to be the day the 120 were in one accord, just as the 120 priests blew trumpets with one accord. As the priests and singers were as one voice, unified, and the glory filled the Temple, we read:

> *Acts 2:1-4 And when the day of Pentecost was fully come, they were all with one accord in one place. And suddenly there came a sound from heaven as of a rushing mighty wind, and it filled all the house where they were sitting. And there appeared unto them cloven tongues like as of fire, and it sat upon each of them. And they were all filled with the Holy*

> Ghost, and began to speak with other tongues, as the Spirit gave them utterance.

The interesting thing about the event was that cloven tongues of fire sat over each of the 120. This same picture is seen in the Tabernacle in the wilderness!

> Exodus 40:33-34 And he reared up the court round about the Tabernacle and the altar, and set up the hanging of the court gate. So Moses finished the work. Then **a cloud covered the tent of the congregation**, and the glory of the LORD filled the Tabernacle.

When the Ark was placed in the holiest of the Tabernacle, the same thing occurred. The glory filled the house, but we also read that the pillar of cloud by day and *fire by night* covered the tent.

> Exodus 40:36-38 And when the cloud was taken up from over the Tabernacle, the children of Israel went onward in all their journeys: But if the cloud were not taken up, then they journeyed not till the day that it was taken up. For the cloud of the LORD was upon the Tabernacle by day, and **fire was on it by night**, in the sight of all the house of Israel, throughout all their journeys.

The pillar was their leader. When we read of the pillars of fire over the heads of the 120 in Acts 2, we are seeing an indication of the TEMPLE or TABERNACLE in the form of the people!

> 1 Corinthians 6:19 What? know ye not that your body is the Temple of the Holy Ghost which is in you, which ye have of God, and ye are not your own?

The fulfillment of the Temple being filled with God's Spirit after the glory of God entered its east gate was a prophecy in vision of the event of returning man in dominion to the Garden once again! This occurred on the day of Pentecost! It already happened!

WASTING THE CHRISTIAN LIFE

When is this going to occur? It has already occurred!

Ezekiel saw a vision of the day of Pentecost when the Church was filled with the Holy Ghost. Israel was a model of the human race redeemed to God. The Temple was a model of the Garden and the palace of man's dominion with God. Jesus Christ is the man upon the throne, the very Glory of God.

> *1 Corinthians 11:7 ...man ...is the image and glory of God:*

> *2 Corinthians 4:6 For God, who commanded the light to shine out of darkness, hath shined in our hearts, to give the light of* **the knowledge of the glory of God in the face of Jesus Christ.**

Those who are pushing everything over into a future heaven are wasting their Christian lives in one sense – they now have dominion and power through Jesus Christ and do not recognize these prophecies as referring to this present reality. There is a heaven to come after this life is over. I believe that. But God never intended us to wait until Heaven to enjoy **dominion**.

> *Revelation 1:6 And hath made us kings and priests unto God and his Father; to him be glory and dominion for ever and ever. Amen.*

Jesus already made us (past tense) kings and priests. We are in the actual Garden right now! It is a spiritual position. If we are waiting for death to go to heaven before we can enjoy victory and dominion, we are wasting our entire Christian lives on earth!

> *Luke 10:19 Behold, I give unto you power to tread on serpents and scorpions, and over all the power of the enemy: and nothing shall by any means hurt you.*

> *Romans 8:31 What shall we then say to these things? If God be for us, who can be against us?*

> *Isaiah 54:17 No weapon that is formed against thee shall prosper; and every tongue that shall rise against thee in judgment thou shalt condemn. This is the heritage of the servants of the LORD, and their righteousness is of me, saith the LORD.*

Jesus died, was buried and has already resurrected from the dead. That is past history. It has been accomplished long ago. After He resurrected, He ascended.

> *Ephesians 1:19-22 And what is the exceeding greatness of his power to us-ward who believe, according to the working of his mighty power, Which he wrought in Christ, when he raised him from the dead, and set him at his own right hand in the heavenly places, Far above all principality, and power, and might, and dominion, and every name that is named, not only in this world, but also in that which is to come: And hath put all things under his feet, and gave him to be the head over all things to the church,*

> *Ephesians 2:5-6 Even when we were dead in sins, hath quickened us together with Christ, (by grace ye are saved;) And hath raised us up together, and made us sit together in heavenly places in Christ Jesus:*

We are presently seated with Christ above all enemies! Presently! It's already done!

Too many believers know nothing about this great victory we have today! But I am glad that the Word of God reveals this to us.

YOU CAN ONLY ENJOY WHAT YOU KNOW IS YOURS

Every one of us may have all the victory anybody can possibly have, but if we do not know it then we will never enjoy it. Paul told us we are seated with Christ above all powers. He preempted that truth by saying this:

> *Ephesians 1:15-18 Wherefore I also, after I heard of your faith in the Lord Jesus, and love unto all the saints, Cease not to give thanks for you, making mention of you in my prayers; That the God of our Lord Jesus Christ, the Father of glory, may give unto you the spirit of wisdom and revelation in the knowledge of him: The eyes of your understanding being enlightened; that ye may know what is the hope of his calling, and what the riches of the glory of his inheritance in the saints,*

We need to have our eyes of understanding opened up to see what is ours. That is why this Bible teaching is so important. When you know what victory you have, you can enjoy it and no longer waste your Christian life away with anything less.

We can enjoy Garden dominion now. Those in it have passed through the flaming sword.

Thank God that there is a dominion we can experience today over all enemies.

4

IN THE PRESENCE OF THE ONE WHO DWELLS IN THE HOLIEST OF HOLIES

> *Revelation 21:22-22:2* And ***I saw no Temple (Greek: NAHOS) therein: for the Lord God Almighty and the Lamb are the Temple (NAHOS) of it.*** *And the city had no need of the sun, neither of the moon, to shine in it: for the glory of God did lighten it, and the Lamb is the light thereof. And the nations of them which are saved shall walk in the light of it: and the kings of the earth do bring their glory and honour into it. And the gates of it shall not be shut at all by day: for there shall be no night there. And they shall bring the glory and honour of the nations into it. And there shall in no wise enter into it any thing that defileth, neither whatsoever worketh abomination, or maketh a lie: but they which are written in the Lamb's book of life. And he shewed me a pure river of water of life, clear as crystal, proceeding out of the throne of God and of the Lamb. In the midst of the street of it, and on either side of the river, was there the Tree of Life, which bare twelve manner of fruits, and yielded her fruit every month: and the leaves of the tree were for the healing of the nations.*

We saw that the New Jerusalem is the true *Church*. When I say *Church*, I do not mean a holy building made by hands, because we read that God and the Lamb dwell in this building. God said He would not dwell in Temples made with hands. *Church* in the Bible refers to the real and true fellowship of Christians in the world. Don't look for a particular denomination. Also remember that not all who call themselves *Christians* are truly Christians.

John said that God and the Lamb are the *Temple* of this *City* (Rev. 21:22). Recall that the word *Temple* here is translated from a Greek word which brings more detailed truth into the open. That word is *Nahos*. This word speaks of the cell in the Temple where the Ark of the Covenant was actually placed, and was distinguished from the rest of the whole enclosure. When we read that God and the Lamb are the *Nahos* of the City, we are reading that God and the lamb are the *Holy of Holies!*

ENTERING THE LAMB'S DEATH

In the land of Egypt, when the death angel was about to destroy all the firstborn, God told the people through Moses to slay a lamb and strike its blood upon the doorposts of their homes. They would be safe from death once they were behind the doorways stained with the lamb's blood. I always rejoiced that this is a picture of getting *into Christ*. John the Baptist called Jesus Christ *the lamb who takes away the sins of the world* (John 1:29). We read about being "in Christ" throughout the New Testament. We can be *in Christ*, the lamb slain. That is illustrated than by showing a picture of people walking through a doorway that was splattered with lamb's blood.

It was as though the Hebrews *walked into the slain lamb* when they passed through the blood-stained doorways of their homes. Entrance is stressed in thinking of *a door*.

The message we receive from this picture is that you have to be *in Christ* if you want to be freed from the destruction of death, as the people were saved from death that night *in their blood-stained doorways* in Goshen. You must also be *in Christ* as Noah was *in the Ark* if you want to be saved from the destruction of death flooding the world.

IN THE PRESENCE OF THE ONE WHO DWELLS IN THE HOLIEST OF HOLIES

When we read Revelation 21, we find further insights as to how the blood-stained doorways *represented entrance* into *the Garden* where a flaming sword would kill the sinful people who entered.

Get the picture. The Lamb died so that the people walking into their houses would not have to die. Similarly, we need to get inside the Garden back to the place in which Adam stood before death became a part of his life when he sinned. They could, therefore, be inside and freed from death. The *Garden* and *the Houses in Egypt* and *the New Jerusalem* all represent the same thing – the Holy of Holies!

It might sound confusing at first. The houses represented the *lamb* and also represented *the Holy of Holies*. How could that be? Must it not be one or the other? But think about it.

Revelation 21:22 says that *God and the Lamb* are the *Nahos* of the city. They comprise the Holy of Holies. That means the Lamb is the Holy of Holies! When we are *in the city*, we are *in the lamb* and inside *the true Holy of Holies*. Jesus is the Holy of Holies!

ATONEMENT UPON THE ARK OF THE COVENANT'S MERCY SEAT

In the Holiest of Holies was the Ark of the Covenant. This was the object upon which God's presence dwelt in that holiest place. It was a chest that contained the tablets of stone engraved with the Ten Commandments. It had a solid gold lid in the shape of a seat with Cherubim on each end, whose faces looked down on the seat and whose wings covered the seat (Exodus 25:17-20). That *seat* was where blood was sprinkled from the atonement sacrifice that was slain (Lev. 16:14). That Blood made *atonement* for their sins. It removed the sins from the people (Lev. 16:16). Blood was put on that particular place of the Ark. That was symbolic of Christ having gone into Heaven and presented God with the payment for the sins that were committed by the people. This was so that these people could be free of death.

This was the only place God's presence dwelt in those days in the Earth. Today, I want to be in the presence of God.

NOTHING BUT THE BLOOD

If they had placed a beautiful bouquet of roses there, God would not dwell there and those roses would not be in the presence of God. Had they walked into that empty room and began to do all the good deeds and say all the good things to each other they could think of, to see if God would move and dwell there because of their good works, God would not have come. He only came where a piece of gold had been beaten by hammers into the shape of Cherubim whose faces looked down to a spot where sacrificial blood was sprinkled.

There were two more rather gigantic forms of cherubim in Solomon's Temple whose wings touched one another (1 Kings 6:27). The ark was situated beneath those huge wings in the most holy place.

In Isaiah we read of the throne of God and God sitting there, high and lifted up. His train, His royal robe, filled the Temple. Around Him were *Seraphim* with six wings. Two wings of the Seraphim covered their faces, two covered their feet and two were used that they might fly (Isaiah 6:1-3). This picture of Seraphim covering the face and feet represented deep humility. The act of covering the face and feet speaks of the realization of how great God is, so that we are *covered in submission* and the greatest of *reverence* to Him. We should not be seen in the Presence of Him alone Who is worthy to be noticed.

The Hebrew term for *Seraphim* literally means *burners*. That reminds us of something.

Two people were on their way to Emmaus, and heard God's word as Jesus, Himself, spoke to them. They later said *their hearts burned* as they talked with Him. This shows us what we need if we want to be among those who can say that they are in God's presence.

IN THE PRESENCE OF THE ONE WHO DWELLS IN THE HOLIEST OF HOLIES

Seraphim show us that if we want to be among those who enter God's deepest place of fellowship, we require deep humility before Him. We must live lives that are honest and sincere. We cover ourselves in our spirits and attitudes, with the spirit of meekness. We are to be in total worship to Him. As the wings covered the place where the *Glory* sat, *we worship Him*.

The wings touched one another. This holiness and real Christianity is manifested amongst people who *join their worship* with others who likewise truly worship Him. We *touch our wings together* when there is no animosity in our hearts against one another, but instead there is only praise and worship for Him. He dwells in the *midst* of two or three in His name.

The term *"in His name"* speaks of the purpose for which we are gathered – it is for Him, for we are His. We do not gather with each other in church services just to put on a show and let others outside the church think we are better than they are. We are the church *if* we are the ones whose hearts are worshipping like wings touching each others' wings – *hearts touching hearts* in union for His will to be done.

UNDERSTANDING HOW HIS BLOOD ALONE IS OUR SALVATION

As the eyes of the Cherubim looked down at the Mercy Seat where the blood was sprinkled, we will not dare to look to anything else – not our good works, nor our beautiful showmanship of how nice we can dress in church. We must look to nothing else aside from the precious shed blood of Jesus as the reason for our existence in His presence!

The blood is the only reason we are saved. It is the only reason we can be in God's presence. The *blood of Jesus* is an embodying term that speaks of all the work of Christ through the death of the cross accomplished in order to save our souls. We are saved by His works, and His works alone.

That blood was sprinkled on a *Mercy Seat*. Nothing but God's *mercy* brought us through.

> *Ephesians 2:1-5 And you hath he quickened, who were dead in trespasses and sins; Wherein in time past ye walked according to the course of this world, according to the prince of the power of the air, the spirit that now worketh in the children of disobedience: Among whom also we all had our conversation in times past in the lusts of our flesh, fulfilling the desires of the flesh and of the mind; and were by nature the children of wrath, even as others. But God,* **who is rich in mercy***, for his great love wherewith he loved us, Even when we were dead in sins, hath quickened us together with Christ, (by grace ye are saved;) And hath raised us up together, and made us sit together in heavenly places in Christ Jesus:*

We must know what it means to be *saved by grace*. We were rescued from *judgment!* We all formerly walked in the filth of the world, no matter how groomed a lifestyle we may have lived. God looked down in love and wanted to deliver and rescue us. He loved us so much that it is said *He raised us up* with the love and power with which He raised up Jesus from the dead. The resurrection is given to us totally by a free gift. It was not done due to our striving to be so good that we were raised with Christ.

The Bible says that while we were dead in trespasses and sins God rescued us. He considered us to be in a state of damnation and death caused by the tragedy of our abundance of sins. How could we have made any score-points by good deeds if God had to save us while He considered us to be in a pit of damnation?

We were so useless as far as rescuing ourselves by good deeds was concerned, to the point that God viewed us as useless as *dead carcases on the ground*, because of our sinfulness. Forget about doing something to save ourselves! How much more useless can one be than in laying on the ground dead?

IN THE PRESENCE OF THE ONE WHO DWELLS IN THE HOLIEST OF HOLIES

Being saved and in the presence of God is nothing that results from *what a* person *can do* to achieve such a position. Without God you are dead in trespasses and sins.

> *Ephesians 2:8-14 For by grace are ye saved through faith; and that not of yourselves: it is the gift of God: Not of works, lest any man should boast. For we are his workmanship, created in Christ Jesus unto good works, which God hath before ordained that we should walk in them. Wherefore remember, that ye being in time past Gentiles in the flesh, who are called Uncircumcision by that which is called the Circumcision in the flesh made by hands; That at that time ye were without Christ, being aliens from the commonwealth of Israel, and strangers from the covenants of promise, having no hope, and without God in the world: But now in Christ Jesus ye who sometimes were far off are made nigh by the blood of Christ. For he is our peace, who hath made both one, and hath broken down the middle wall of partition between us;*

"Wherefore remember..." What powerful words! The eyes of the Cherubim looking down on the Mercy Seat symbolized hearts of believers washed by that blood *who always remember what it was that saved* them. They know that the blood of Jesus alone has saved them. So, their eyes always gaze upon it. This represents the people who dwell in the Holiest.

No one but those who are cleansed and, also *(always keep in mind what saved* them*)*, *are the people who* dwell in the holiest with the One who dwells there.

The vision so shook Isaiah in Isaiah chapter 6, that he cried out...

> *Isaiah 6:5 Then said I, Woe is me! for I am undone; because I am a man of unclean lips, and I dwell in the midst of a people of unclean lips: for mine eyes saw the King, the LORD of hosts.*

What fear of God was inspired in the heart of Isaiah when he caught a glimpse of this most holy sanctuary!
THIS IS THE CHURCH.
THIS IS THE HOLIEST OF THE HOLIES.
THIS IS THE NEW JERUSALEM.

THE CHURCH, THE CITY ON THE MOUNTAIN

Jesus went to prepare a place for us. He went to build a City. Abraham looked for *a City* whose builder and maker is God. Jesus reiterated the origin of that City when He said "Upon this rock I will build my church."

Notice the pattern...

> *Genesis 2:21-24 And the LORD God caused a deep sleep to fall upon Adam, and he slept: and he took one of his ribs, and closed up the flesh instead thereof; And the rib, which the LORD God had taken from man, made he a woman, and brought her unto the man. And Adam said, This is now bone of my bones, and flesh of my flesh: she shall be called Woman, because she was taken out of Man. Therefore shall a man leave his father and his mother, and shall cleave unto his wife: and they shall be one flesh.*

1. God put Adam in a sleep.
2. God removed material from inside Adam.
3. God used the material and *"made"* (Hebr. BANAH – built) the woman.

Banah is defined as *to build, build up,* and *make*. It is *to establish,* or to *cause to* continue. It also is used in the sense of *building a house*. God literally *built* the woman. We miss this sense of the term in the English version of the verse. As the woman was *in Adam* before she was actually made, we were chosen *in Christ before the foundation of the world* (Eph. 1:4). The book of Ephesians

IN THE PRESENCE OF THE ONE WHO DWELLS IN THE HOLIEST OF HOLIES

gives us the same pattern of God's work in making the church as Genesis does of making Eve.

> *Ephesians 1:4 According as he hath chosen us in him before the foundation of the world, that we should be holy and without blame before him in love:*

We were in Him before the foundation of the world. Then we read in chapter 2 of the same book a mention of the salvation from a world of sin that we must never forget.

> *Ephesians 2:17-19 And came and preached peace to you which were afar off, and to them that were nigh. For through him we both have access by one Spirit unto the Father. Now therefore ye are no more strangers and foreigners, but fellowcitizens with the saints, and of the household of God;*

We are said to be *the household of God*. We are no longer strangers. We are *the city* and *the Temple* of God.

And then we come to something else most wonderful in Ephesians:

> *Ephesians 2:20-22 And are built upon the foundation of the apostles and prophets, Jesus Christ himself being the chief corner stone; In whom all the building fitly framed together groweth unto an holy Temple in the Lord: In whom ye also are builded together for an habitation of God through the Spirit.*

The above tells us that we are actually God's house that is *built up*, as the woman was *banah* (built) by God. He took the materials to *build* her from within Adam.

Notice another detail we find in Ephesians:

Ephesians 4:8 Wherefore he saith, When he ascended up on high, he led captivity captive, and gave gifts unto men.

Why did Christ ascend? Was it not to prepare a place for us (John 14:2-3)? Christ told the disciples that He had to go in order to prepare *a place* for them. He had to ascend to the Father to accomplish this. Here in Ephesians we read that He also ascended to give gifts to men. Why?

Ephesians 4:11-13 And he gave some, apostles; and some, prophets; and some, evangelists; and some, pastors and teachers; **For the perfecting of the saints, for the work of the ministry, for the edifying of the body of Christ:** *Till we all come in the unity of the faith, and of the knowledge of the Son of God, unto a perfect man, unto the measure of the stature of the fulness of Christ:*

He gave gifts to the church for the purpose of *building us up*. To construct our lives!

THE CHURCH, THE NEW EVE

Church, we are meant to minister to one another. The preacher preaches... The teacher teaches... The prophet prophesies.... And so on. We are given these gifts so we can get to work and *edify the Body of the Church*.

The woman was going to *help* Adam *dress and keep* the Garden once she was created and by his side. She would build the Garden up with Adam. The picture of the woman being *built* from materials taken from Adam is identical to the manner in which God chose to *build the Church*. We were said to be *in Christ* before the foundation of the world, just as the woman was essentially in Adam before she walked the world. Gift ministries of the Spirit are given to continue to *build up*, or edify, the Church. What an *edifice* this Church of God's people really is!

IN THE PRESENCE OF THE ONE WHO DWELLS IN THE HOLIEST OF HOLIES

The people of God, the Church, are the *City* that is *built by God*. *The* Bride of Christ, as the woman was Adam's bride after having herself been built by God, is the New Jerusalem Abraham looked for. The New Jerusalem is not a literal physical City of buildings and actual golden streets, but is a symbol of the *Church*, the *Bride, built by God*.

Jesus referred to the people as *His Church*. The word *church* means *called*-out *ones*. He said He would *build* His *called-out* ones on *a rock*. He referred to them as a structure built on a foundation. This is clearly what Revelation referred to, using the same symbolism Jesus used to tell us *the Church is the city*! The Church is the Holy of Holies! It is the *Nahos!* Thank God that we can dwell with the One who dwells in the Holiest of Holies!

5

A Place In The Holiest of Holies

Only two things in the Bible were ever made in the form of a perfect *cube*.

1. The New Jerusalem.

2. The Holiest of Holies, also called the *Oracle* of the Temple.

Revelation 21:9-11 And there came unto me one of the seven angels which had the seven vials full of the seven last plagues, and talked with me, saying, Come hither, I will shew thee the bride, the Lamb's wife. And he carried me away in the spirit to a great and high mountain, and shewed me that great city, the holy Jerusalem, descending out of heaven from God, Having the glory of God: and her light was like unto a stone most precious, even like a jasper stone, clear as crystal;

Revelation 21:16 And the city lieth foursquare, and the length is as large as the breadth: and he measured the city with the reed, twelve thousand furlongs. The length and the breadth and the height of it are equal.

A PLACE IN THE HOLIEST OF HOLIES

Revelation 22:1-2 And he shewed me a pure river of water of life, clear as crystal, proceeding out of the throne of God and of the Lamb. In the midst of the street of it, and on either side of the river, was there the Tree of Life, which bare twelve manner of fruits, and yielded her fruit every month: and the leaves of the tree were for the healing of the nations.

1 Kings 6:19-20 And the oracle he prepared in the house within, to set there the Ark of the covenant of the LORD. And the oracle in the forepart was twenty cubits in length, and twenty cubits in breadth, and twenty cubits in the height thereof: and he overlaid it with pure gold; and so covered the altar which was of cedar.

Each of these two things was connected, as we saw, with the thought of returning man into the Garden of Eden. The Bible is full of such illustrations that reveal a message about how God works with the world and people for their salvation.

THE GARDEN, THE TEMPLE & THE NEW JERUSALEM

The New Jerusalem along with the Garden of Eden had the Tree of Life in it (Gen 2:9; Rev. 22:1). The Holiest of Holies in the Temple (1 Kings 6) had a barrier of Cherubim as did the Garden of Eden. Instead of the Tree of Life, the Holiest contained the Ark of the Covenant.

If you look at a map of old Jerusalem in the time of the temple, you will find that the Temple was placed *in the same position in the City of Jerusalem as the Garden was placed in Eden* – EASTWARD. Clearly the Temple represents the Garden.

The Garden, the Holiest and the New Jerusalem all speak about the same desired goal of God. God wants us to be inside a most holy place where there is eternal Life, and where sin cannot enter and have dominion. Adam lived there but had to leave because of sin.

Recall that when God created Adam, He told him to dress and keep the Garden. He was to protect it from invaders and from sin. But Adam failed, and a serpent found its way inside. The serpent caused Adam to sin and he and his wife had to be removed. The Bible teaches that all of creation fell into bondage because of that event.

> *Romans 8:20-22 For the creature was made subject to vanity, not willingly, but by reason of him who hath subjected the same in hope, Because the creature itself also shall be delivered from the bondage of corruption into the glorious liberty of the children of God. For we know that the whole creation groaneth and travaileth in pain together until now.*

Notice that all of creation fell with Adam and Eve. But one thing did not fall with them. The Garden did not fall. How could the entire creation fall into bondage with Adam while the Garden of Eden didn't?

One thing we know is that the Garden was not like the rest of creation. It seems to have been something that was partially physical and partially spiritual. It was the place where heaven joined earth, so to speak.

The details of places and objects in the Genesis story of the Garden can be seen to be like seeds which are planted there and begin to grow throughout the rest of the Bible. For this reason, men have often called the first eleven chapters of Genesis *The Seed Plot of the Bible*. By the time we read through to the book of Revelation, these things are fully *grown* and *harvested*.

Notice that New Jerusalem has the same Tree of Life that the Garden had, but with *walls* around it. The Garden was also enclosed, for we read that God placed Cherubim and a sword as *keepers* of the Garden in the east side, and did not place them anywhere else around the Garden. Obviously the Garden was an enclosed sanctuary with an eastern entrance.

A PLACE IN THE HOLIEST OF HOLIES

I Go to Prepare a Place For You

Adam failed to *keep* (or protect and guard) the Garden, and the serpent entered in. Adam was then cast out and the Garden was sealed off from him!

However, thanks be to God, Jesus came to fix up the damage caused by Adam, and to redeem mankind as well. There was a place into which we could not enter since we left Eden, and Jesus came to do something about it!

> *John 7:34 Ye shall seek me, and shall not find me: and where I am, thither ye cannot come.*
>
> *John 7:36 What manner of saying is this that he said, Ye shall seek me, and shall not find me: and where I am, thither ye cannot come?*
>
> *John 8:21 Then said Jesus again unto them, I go my way, and ye shall seek me, and shall die in your sins: whither I go, ye cannot come.*
>
> *John 13:33 Little children, yet a little while I am with you. Ye shall seek me: and as I said unto the Jews, Whither I go, ye cannot come; so now I say to you.*

Notice the number of times Jesus spoke of his departure to a place that the people could not come.

And then He made this statement:

> *John 14:2-3 In my Father's house are many mansions: if it were not so, I would have told you. I go to prepare a place for you. And if I go and prepare a place for you, I will come again, and receive you unto myself; that where I am, there ye may be also.*

We could not go there. But Jesus said He was going to go there in order to *make a way* for *us so we would have a place there.* This is talking about none other than the place that the story of the Garden of Eden tried to relate to us in Genesis. The New Jerusalem is *that place*! This is where the Tree of Life is found again!

Note that Revelation 21 said that nothing enters there that is sinful:

> *Revelation 21:27 And there shall in no wise enter into it any thing that defileth, neither whatsoever worketh abomination, or maketh a lie: but they which are in the Lamb's book of life.*

When we see the New Jerusalem with walls around the Tree of Life, we see the structure Adam was supposed to eventually construct, but was instead built by Jesus Christ! Had Adam not sinned, we can imagine a city being built by him to house all the people born from his marriage to Eve.

Jesus made a way for us to enter into this Holy of Holies!

THE WAY & THE PLACE

Notice how Jesus described the details about preparing a place for them.

> *John 14:2-7 In my Father's house are many mansions: if it were not so, I would have told you. I go to prepare a place for you. And if I go and prepare a place for you, I will come again, and receive you unto myself; that where I am, there ye may be also. And whither I go ye know, and the way ye know. Thomas saith unto him, Lord, we know not whither thou goest; and how can we know the way? Jesus saith unto him, I am the way, the truth, and the life: no man cometh unto the Father, but by me. If ye had known me, ye should*

A PLACE IN THE HOLIEST OF HOLIES

have known my Father also: and from henceforth ye know him, and saw him.

He said the place to which He was going was a place of which they knew. He also said they knew *the way* to get there.

When they asked Him what He meant, He said *the place* is *with the Father*, and *the way is the Son*, Jesus Christ. Jesus *is* the way. The destination is fellowship with the Father.

Recall that the Father was in the Garden, where He walked with Adam.

Jesus said He *was* going to prepare a place for us where we once were when we were within Adam's loins before his fall.

Jesus was going to the place where the Father was.

*John 14:12 Verily, verily, I say unto you, He that believeth on me, the works that I do shall he do also; and greater works than these shall he do; because **I go unto my Father**.*

WHAT EXACTLY IS THIS PLACE?

When will He prepare this place for us? Now? Could it already be *done*? Or is it *being done*? Is that place finished yet? When will it be finished?

We hear this passage of scripture read many times at funerals as though the construction of this place is not yet finished. But notice what the rest of the chapter says.

John 14:18 -19 I will not leave you comfortless: I will come to you. Yet a little while, and the world seeth me no more; but ye see me:

This really puzzled the disciples. What did He mean, *"The world would* not see *Him, but they would"*?

There stood Jesus speaking about leaving and returning, as He spoke in the first few verses of the chapter. Make a mental note of this fact.

Then Jesus spoke again and Judas asked a question. Watch the conversation carefully.

> *John 14:21-23 He that hath my commandments, and keepeth them, he it is that loveth me: and he that loveth me shall be loved of my Father, and I will love him, and will manifest myself to him. Judas saith unto him, not Iscariot, Lord,* **how is it that thou wilt manifest thyself unto us, and not unto the world?** *Jesus answered and said unto him,* **If a man love me, he will keep my words: and my Father will love him, and we will come unto him, and make our abode with him.**

Judas asked how they would see Him while the rest of the world would not. He gave us a hint when he said *He would not leave us comfortless but would come to us.* Then He said He and the Father would come and make their abode *with us.* There is the key! (The Greek term translated as "abode" is the same word translated as "mansions" in this chapter in verse 2!)

There is one other place where God spoke of making a *dwelling place,* or *an abode,* among men.

> *Exodus 25:8 And let them make me a sanctuary; that I may dwell among them.*

The Tabernacle and the Temple! This is all connected together.

He would leave the disciples and make *a place* for *them,* and return as *the* Comforter and make His *abode* with them.

We said that the Garden of Eden was like a Sanctuary, preserved for holy things and holy people. It was the pattern for the Tabernacle and Temple. The Garden was the true Holy of Holies. Man once dwelt there in Adam, and walked with God the Father. But man sinned and had to leave.

God Himself came as another *Adam* in order to undo the damage the first Adam caused, and to redeem man again so man could return into that sanctuary. He built the walls. He made many mansions in there. After He said He would prepare a place, He said He would return to them **and the world would not see Him but His disciples would see Him**. He indicated that it was to the Father He was going. They could not yet go there with Him, but they would have a place there soon enough.

When He said His return would cause Him to be One who would not leave them comfortless, but would indeed return to them – I ask you – was this something that has not yet happened as of this day?

He said He and the Father would come to them and *make their abode with them*, as though they would become the Temple. Has that happened yet?

> *1Corinthians 6:19 What? know ye not that your body is the Temple of the Holy Ghost which is in you, which ye have of God, and ye are not your own?*

> *Ephesians 2:20-22 And are built upon the foundation of the apostles and prophets, Jesus Christ himself being the chief corner stone; In whom all the building fitly framed together groweth unto an holy Temple in the Lord: In whom ye also are builded together for an habitation of God through the Spirit.*

> *1Pet 2:5 Ye also, as lively stones, are built up a spiritual house, an holy priesthood, to offer up spiritual sacrifices, acceptable to God by Jesus Christ.*

I think this has already happened! Jesus indicated to Peter He was about to prepare a place for them and it was not yet done at the time in which He spoke.

> *Matthew 16:18 And I say also unto thee, That thou art Peter, and upon this rock I will build my church; and the gates of hell shall not prevail against it.*

Did he already do it since then? How did He go to the Father? When did He go to the Father? What did He mean that He was soon going to leave and they could not go with Him?

He went by way of the death, burial, resurrection, and ascension!

He gave us a hint *when* he would return and *how* he would return.

> *John 14:16-18 And I will pray the Father, and he shall give you another Comforter, that he may abide with you for ever; Even the Spirit of truth; whom the world cannot receive, because it seeth him not, neither knoweth him: but ye know him; for he dwelleth with you, and shall be in you. I will not leave you comfortless: I will come to you.*
>
> *John 14:26 But the Comforter, which is the Holy Ghost...*

The Holy Ghost was given to the Church after this. He certainly did not leave us comfortless! The Comforter indeed did come! *The Comforter is the Holy Ghost.*

He spoke of the people being made the Church as though they were a Tabernacle. With that in mind, notice what we read about the New Jerusalem.

> *Revelation 21:2-3 And I John saw the holy city, new Jerusalem, coming down from God out of heaven, prepared as a bride adorned for her husband. And I heard a great voice out of heaven saying, Behold,* **the Tabernacle of God is with men***, and he will dwell with them, and they shall be his people, and God himself shall be with them, and be their God.*

The bride is *the Tabernacle of God with men*. The church is the Temple of the Holy Ghost. We are now in the New Jerusalem!

> *Galatians 4:26 But Jerusalem* **which is above is free,** *which is the mother of us all.*

Is this not written in the present tense? Is it not written as if this New Jerusalem is already built?

> *Hebrews 12:22-23 But* **ye are come** *unto mount Sion, and* **unto the city of the living God, the heavenly Jerusalem**, *and to an innumerable company of angels, To the general assembly and church of the firstborn, which are written in heaven, and to God the Judge of all, and to the spirits of just men made perfect,*

WE WILL MAKE OUR ABODE

Jesus said He was *the way* to the Father. He said we would be *with the* Father and *with Him* when He prepared a place for us and returned to abide among us. That is the reason you read of the throne of God and of the Lamb that is found in the City. The throne is there for both God and the Lamb. Father and the Son. They *both* abide in this city, just as Jesus said:

> *John 14:23 Jesus answered and said unto him, If a man love me, he will keep my words: and my Father will love him, and* **we will come unto him, and make our abode with him.**

> *Revelation 22:1 And he shewed me a pure river of water of life, clear as crystal, proceeding out of the* **throne of God and of the Lamb.**

Notice that John invites people to come right now:

> *Revelation 22:16-17 I Jesus have sent mine angel to testify unto you these things in the churches. I am the root and the offspring of David, and the bright and morning star. And the*

> *Spirit and the bride say, Come. And let him that heareth say, Come. And let him that is athirst come. And whosoever will, let him take the water of life freely.*

He did not say *wait* for a time in the future when you will be able to come. He said we can come right now and taste of the water of life freely. Where is the water of life?

> *Revelation 22:1 And he shewed me a pure river of water of life, clear as crystal, proceeding out of the throne of God and of the Lamb.*

If we can come and drink of the water of life now, and the water of life flows out of the city from the throne, then the City is a *now* thing. The City is already in existence. The City is the Church.

> *Matthew 5:14* **Ye are** *the light of the world.* **A city** *that is set on an hill cannot be hid.*

WE ARE THE CITY

They sing a song that goes like this:

There's a country far beyond the starry sky,
There's a city where there never comes a night.

No. There's a city right here right now that is not beyond the starry sky. We have already *come* to the Heavenly Jerusalem. We are the Tabernacle, or the Temple of God.
Hello, Temple! Hello, City!
The Comforter has come and the Father and the Son have made their abode with us! God is in us!
Jesus rose from the tomb and told Mary not to touch Him for He had not yet *ascended to the Father*. By telling Mary to not

A PLACE IN THE HOLIEST OF HOLIES

touch Him, He spoke of going to the Father as the High Priest would go into the Holiest of Holies.

> *Leviticus 16:17 And there shall be no man in the Tabernacle of the congregation when he goeth in to make an atonement in the holy place, until he come out, and have made an atonement for himself, and for his household, and for all the congregation of Israel.*

In Revelation we see the Lamb going into the Holiest, into the Garden, into the *City* where the *throne of God stood*.

> *Revelation 4:2 And immediately I was in the spirit: and, behold, a throne was set in heaven, and one sat on the throne.*

> *Revelation 5:6-7 And I beheld, and, lo, in the midst of the throne and of the four beasts, and in the midst of the elders, stood a Lamb as it had been slain, having seven horns and seven eyes, which are the seven Spirits of God sent forth into all the earth. And he came and took the book out of the right hand of him that sat upon the throne.*

He went to the Father to prepare a place for us. In what manner did He enter? As the High Priest going into the Holiest to make atonement for the sins of the people, Jesus went to Heaven to the Father to make *Atonement* for our sins.

> *Romans 5:11 And not only so, but we also joy in God through our Lord Jesus Christ, by whom we have now received the atonement.*

Notice the wording here. *We have now received the atonement.* The high priest entered the Holiest to make atonement. Jesus talked to Mary as though He was going into the holiest when no one could touch Him. Paul said we have atonement *now*. Jesus already went and returned!

When the Lamb took the book, notice what was said.

Revelation 5:9 And they sung a new song, saying, Thou art worthy to take the book, and to open the seals thereof: **for thou wast slain, and hast redeemed us to God by thy blood** *out of every kindred, and tongue, and people, and nation;*

The conclusion of the matter is that Jesus did the work, then His Spirit came back, and the Church was born and built on the Rock.

It is *done*!

6

A PLACE FOR YOU AT GOD'S THRONE

Exodus 24:1-2 And he said unto Moses, **Come up unto the LORD***, thou, and Aaron, Nadab, and Abihu, and seventy of the elders of Israel; and worship ye afar off. And Moses alone shall come near the LORD: but they shall not come nigh; neither shall the people go up with him.*

Exodus 24:9 -10 Then went up Moses, and Aaron, Nadab, and Abihu, and seventy of the elders of Israel: And they saw the God of Israel: and there was under his feet as it were a paved work of a sapphire stone, and as it were the body of heaven in his clearness.

Exodus 24:12-13 And the LORD said unto Moses, Come up to me into the mount, and be there: and I will give thee tables of stone, and a law, and commandments which I have written; that thou mayest teach them. And Moses rose up, and his minister Joshua: and Moses went up into the mount of God.

Exodus 24:15-18 And Moses went up into the mount, and a cloud covered the mount. And the glory of the LORD abode upon mount Sinai, and the cloud covered it six days: and the seventh day he called un to Moses out of the midst of

> the cloud. *And the sight of the glory of the LORD was like devouring fire on the top of the mount in the eyes of the children of Israel. And Moses went into the midst of the cloud, and gat him up into the mount: and Moses was in the mount forty days and forty nights.*
>
> *Revelation 4:1-2 After this I looked, and, behold, a door was opened in heaven: and the first voice which* **I heard was as it were of a trumpet talking with me; which said, Come up hither,** *and I will shew thee things which must be hereafter. And immediately I was in the spirit: and, behold, a throne was set in heaven, and one sat on the throne.*

The redemption of the people of God by the Blood of Jesus is the greatest work that mankind could ever know. It fully restored what we lost in Eden, reinstating us as kings and priests to God. If we can see that we are seated with Him, and that there is power that presently works in us, we will understand the Kingdom of God accurately.

Paul wrote of his desire for the Ephesians to have a revelation of what is the greatness of God's power toward us, what we have going for us who believe, according to the power He used when He raised Christ from the dead and set Him at his right hand. That power God wrought in Christ is the power for *us*. All this power is *towards us*, Paul said. Can we see it, though?

> *Ephesians 1:17-20 That the God of our Lord Jesus Christ, the Father of glory, may give unto you the spirit of wisdom and revelation in the knowledge of him: The eyes of your understanding being enlightened; that ye may know what is the hope of his calling, and what the riches of the glory of his inheritance in the saints,* **And what is the exceeding greatness of his power to us-ward** *who believe, according to the working of his mighty power, Which he wrought in Christ, when he raised him from the dead, and set him at his own right hand in the heavenly places,*

Then we read:

> *Ephesians 2:5-6 Even when we were dead in sins, hath quickened us together with Christ, (by grace ye are saved;) And hath raised us up together, and made us sit together in heavenly places in Christ Jesus:*

This is the same power that was wrought in Christ when God raised Him from the dead. The revelation of this truth is aptly found in the biblical book entitled after that effect – the Book of the Revelation of Jesus Christ.

To what better book should we go in order to receive *a revelation* of the power for us, who believe, according to the power wrought in Christ when God raised him from the dead?

We are raised together with Jesus Christ.

We are right now seated with Him in heavenly places.

FAITH

In the Bible, we read overcomers are to sit with Christ.

> *Revelation 3:21* **To him that overcometh will I grant to sit with me** *in my throne, even as I also overcame, and am set down with my Father in his throne.*

Surely all of us want to enjoy this seating. So, how is it that we overcome?

> *1 John 5:4 For whatsoever is born of God overcometh the world: and this is the victory that overcometh the world, even our faith.*

Entering a place of faith with Christ, which seats you with Him, is entering eldership. You cease from your own works and *rest* in His finished work.

Hebrews 4:10 For he that is entered into his rest, he also hath ceased from his own works, as God did from his.

Hebrews 10:12-14 But this man, after he had offered one sacrifice for sins for ever, sat down on the right hand of God; From henceforth expecting till his enemies be made his footstool. For by one offering he hath perfected for ever them that are sanctified.

He did His work and we are to sit with Him. His single offering of Himself in death did the entire job! When battles come, we are not meant to worry, but sit. Know that the work is already done. Don't worry about the enemy bringing trials. He has already been defeated by the blood. There will be some mopping up later on, but for now God has him in check and control. He does nothing God will not allow him to do. Christ is seated above all principalities. So when battles come, remember that God is in control.

Take it from Paul. Paul was content in any state he was in – he rested and was seated with Christ.

WE HAVE THE REAL TEMPLE

In Revelation 5, John saw the actual Temple of Heaven.

The Temple John saw was what Moses also saw so long ago when God gave him the pattern! Moses built a model of it in the world and called it the Tabernacle. Later we read of a fuller-scaled model called the Temple. But in both cases, they only had a model of the true. *We have the real thing!*

The first thing John saw correlates perfectly with the first thing Moses saw after he saw the sapphire pavement where he and Joshua, Aaron, and seventy elders saw God and ate and supped with Him (Ex. 24:10).

A PLACE FOR YOU AT GOD'S THRONE

MOSES

Exodus 25:8-10 And let them make me a sanctuary; that I may dwell among them. According to all that I shew thee, after the pattern of the Tabernacle, and the pattern of all the instruments thereof, even so shall ye make it. And they shall make an **Ark** *of shittim wood: two cubits and a half shall be the length thereof, and a cubit and a half the breadth thereof, and a cubit and a half the height thereof.*

JOHN

Revelation 4:2 And immediately I was in the spirit: and, behold, a **throne was set in heaven**, *and one sat on the throne.*

MOSES

Exodus 25:23 Thou shalt **also make a table** *of shittim wood: two cubits shall be the length thereof, and a cubit the breadth thereof, and a cubit and a half the height thereof.*

v. 30 And thou shalt **set upon the table shewbread** *before me alway.*

Leviticus 24:5 And thou shalt take fine flour, and bake twelve cakes thereof: two tenth deals shall be in one cake.

JOHN

Revelation 4:4 And round about the throne were **four and twenty seats**: *and upon the seats I saw four and twenty elders sitting, clothed in white raiment; and they had on their heads crowns of gold.*

MOSES

*Exodus 25:31-32 And thou shalt **make a candlestick of pure gold**: of beaten work shall the candlestick be made: his shaft, and his branches, his bowls, his knops, and his flowers, shall be of the same. And six branches shall come out of the sides of it;* **three branches of the candlestick out of the one side, and three branches of the candlestick out of the other side:**

JOHN

Revelation 4:5 And out of the throne proceeded lightnings and thunderings and voices: and **there were seven lamps of fire** *burning before the throne, which are the seven Spirits of God.*

MOSES

Exodus 26:31 And thou shalt make a vail of blue, and purple, and scarlet, and fine twined linen of cunning work: with cherubims shall it be made:

JOHN

Revelation 4:6 And before the throne there was a sea of glass like unto crystal: and in the midst of the throne, and round about the throne, were four beasts full of eyes before and behind.

GOD'S THRONE

John saw the same throne room Moses saw. Moses made a pattern of it when he made the Tabernacle. The first thing Moses was shown was the *throne* and God told him to make a replica of it in the form of *the Ark of the Covenant*.

John also saw the throne first. John heard God call, "Come up hither," just as Moses heard God call, "Come up unto the Lord."

24 ELDERS

After the throne, the second sight John saw was of twenty four elders sitting on twenty four seats. In Moses' case, after the mention of the Ark with its Mercy Seat throne, Moses was told to make a table of shewbread. We only find twelve pieces of bread later on in this Tabernacle. Why do we see twenty four elders seated if the table of shewbread with twelve loaves corresponds to the twenty four seats in Revelation? We know that we are seated together with Jesus in heavenly places, and therefore this picture of elders seated around the throne refers to us, somehow. But why twenty four? There were only twelve tribes of Israel in the Old Testament during Moses' time.

However, since that time, there have not only been twelve tribes of God's people, but also twelve apostles. So twelve from the Order of God in the Old Testament and twelve from the order in the New Testament adds up to twenty four!

There are not actually twenty four people sitting with Christ around the throne today, but all those under the order of the Old Testament and those under the order of the New Testament are represented. All Old Testament saints and New Testament saints combined make this grand *people of God*.

Take note that the twenty four seats are the second thing mentioned in John's vision after he saw the throne of God. Church, God has your place mentioned second to His throne in Heaven because He wants to fellowship with you. None other are more important than His saints to Him! We are a blessed people! When the Priests ate the shewbread in the Tabernacle, they were supping with God!

Revelation 3:20-21 Behold, I stand at the door, and knock: if any man hear my voice, and open the door, I will come in to him, and will sup with him, and he with me. To him that overcometh will I grant to sit with me in my throne, even as I also overcame, and am set down with my Father in his throne.

We sit with Christ and eat with Him. We fellowship. When life gets hard and the storms break across the bows of our ships, we can sit with Christ knowing He has it all in control. After a hard day's work, we can sit down with Jesus and sup with Him and talk it over!

Then John saw something similar, but much greater than what Moses experienced.

SEVEN LAMPS OF FIRE

Moses was then told to make *a candlestick of seven lamps* – a shaft with six branches coming out from its sides. John saw the seven lamps of fire by the throne of God.

SEA OF GLASS AND THE BEASTS

Fourthly, Moses was told to make a veil with Cherubim in it. John then saw a sea of glass with four beasts, and Revelation 4:7 tells us they looked like the Cherubim Ezekiel saw in Ezekiel 1 and Ezekiel 10. The sea of glass prohibited any from getting to the throne as the veil in the Holiest of Holies prohibited anyone from getting to the Ark.

THE TABLETS OF LAW AND
THE SEVEN-SEALED SCROLL

MOSES

Exodus 31:18 And he gave unto Moses, when he had made an end of communing with him upon mount Sinai, two tables of testimony, tables of stone, written with the finger of God.

A PLACE FOR YOU AT GOD'S THRONE

Exodus 32:15 And Moses turned, and went down from the mount, and the two tables of the testimony were in his hand: the tables were written on both their sides; on the one side and on the other were they written.

JOHN

Revelation 5:1 And I saw in the right hand of him that sat on the throne a book written within and on the backside, sealed with seven seals.

We continue in Revelation:

Revelation 5:5-10 And one of the elders saith unto me, Weep not: behold, the Lion of the tribe of Juda, the Root of David, hath prevailed to open the book, and to loose the seven seals thereof. And I beheld, and, lo, in the midst of the throne and of the four beasts, and in the midst of the elders, stood a Lamb as it had been slain, having seven horns and seven eyes, which are the seven Spirits of God sent forth into all the earth. And he came and took the book out of the right hand of him that sat upon the throne. And when he had taken the book, the four beasts and four and twenty elders fell down before the Lamb, having every one of them harps, and golden vials full of odours, which are the prayers of saints. And they sung a new song, saying, Thou art worthy to take the book, and to open the seals thereof: for thou wast slain, and hast redeemed us to God by thy blood out of every kindred, and tongue, and people, and nation; And hast made us unto our God kings and priests: and we shall reign on the earth.

John saw the LAMB take the book.
And when the Lamb took it, the 24 elders and cherubim said "Thou hast redeemed us and made us kings and priests and we shall reign in the earth." Do we realize what this is saying? The Lamb had been slain and resurrected. It *stood* as if it had *been*

slain. This is Jesus' death and resurrection for our sins. This resurrection and presentation of His blood is seen in Revelation 5 symbolically, telling us that He entered the Holiest of Holies and redeemed us with the atoning blood of Himself. That atonement worked restoration to all Adam lost in Eden for us. He made them priests to be able to come before Him whenever they had need and to also worship in His presence. He made the kings to rule on earth in circumstances, overcome the devil and rule their spirits.

THE REVELATION OF WHAT?

Ask yourself, "Why did God give this revelation to John?" Of what is it a revelation?

Revelation 1:1 The Revelation of Jesus Christ...

It is JESUS REVEALED.
It is not a revelation of the endtimes, although it may involve that. It is not a revelation of the antichrist, although it may involve that. It is not even a revelation of what Jesus will do with the world, although that comes into view. It is a revelation of JESUS CHRIST. If we can see where Jesus is, then we can see where we are, for we are raised together with Him in heavenly places. We are *in Christ*. To get a revelation of what He did for us and where He is will help us understand what we have going for us.

Jesus went to the right hand to take the book.
Ephesians says He is seated there. We are seated with Him.
Revelation says He received seven things when he received the book and was seated.

Revelation 5:12 Saying with a loud voice, Worthy is the Lamb that was slain to receive power, and riches, and wisdom, and strength, and honour, and glory, and blessing.

A PLACE FOR YOU AT GOD'S THRONE

1. Power
2. Riches
3. Wisdom
4. Strength
5. Honour
6. Glory
7. Blessing

Seven implies the thought of *"all"* in the Bible.

He has everything we need for our help and salvation!

People are worried about antichrist in the Book of Revelation. It's all been taken care of. God spoke of letting the devil loose for a season. We have it made right now! It's okay. You might be suffering trials, but Jesus prevailed and sits on the throne. If you can relax and believe it, you are sitting there, too. There is a place of rest for you at the throne!

God showed us many strange events through many marvellous visions that would come into the world throughout Revelation. But before all of that, He first showed us Jesus high above every principality and dominion. This is significant. It is so that we would always keep in mind that He has everything in control no matter how bad things look. He still reigns. When trials come before you, remember where you are seated. Nothing can ever get out of control. He is at the right hand of God and so are you! Everything is going to be all right! It has already been taken care of.

7

BARRIER OF KNOWLEDGE, PATHWAY OF LOVE

We must understand the true approach to God, and how one may unknowingly pursue Him through very incorrect means. The problem of legalism that is so common today, we will discover, is based upon a principle which originally threw all mankind into sin. Instead of living by Life, many believers are ignorantly thriving on the principle of the Knowledge of Good and Evil!

Genesis 2:16-17 And the LORD God commanded the man, saying, Of every tree of the Garden thou mayest freely eat: But of the Tree of the Knowledge of Good and Evil, thou shalt not eat of it: for in the day that thou eatest thereof thou shalt surely die.

Hebrews 6:19-20 Which hope we have as an anchor of the soul, both sure and stedfast, and **which entereth into that within the veil**; *Whither the forerunner is for us entered, even Jesus, made an high priest for ever after the order of Melchisedec.*

Ephesus 3:13-19 Wherefore I desire that ye faint not at my tribulations for you, which is your glory. For this cause I bow

BARRIER OF KNOWLEDGE, PATHWAY OF LOVE

my knees unto the Father of our Lord Jesus Christ, Of whom the whole family in heaven and earth is named, That he would grant you, according to the riches of his glory, to be strengthened with might by his Spirit in the inner man; That Christ may dwell in your hearts by faith; that ye, being rooted and grounded in love, May be able to comprehend with all saints what is the breadth, and length, and depth, and height; **And to know the love of Christ, which passeth knowledge, that ye might be filled with all the fulness of God.**

These three passages of Scripture all relate in speaking of one of the most fundamental issues in Christianity and knowing God. The subject goes back to the very beginning of man's fall from fellowship with God. It stretches to span throughout all ages until Christ returns to take actual possession of His purchased Church at the end.

LIVING BY ONE OF TWO TREES

Two fundamental ways of life are portrayed from the beginning in the Garden of Eden. They are represented by two Trees – the Tree of Life and the Tree of the Knowledge of Good and Evil. All of human life can be categorized under one of these two trees. After Adam fell and until the time of Christ, though, only one of the two manners of life was experienced. That was life based upon the principle of the Tree of the Knowledge of Good and Evil.

Let me explain.

Genesis 3:23-24 Therefore the LORD God sent him forth from the Garden of Eden, to till the ground from whence he was taken. So he drove out the man; and he placed at the east of the Garden of Eden Cherubims, and a flaming sword which turned every way, to keep the way of the Tree of Life.

God placed a barrier of cherubim at the single Garden entrance to bar man out after God cast him out. This was because Adam and Eve had eaten of the Tree of the Knowledge of Good and Evil. That life force was then inside the couple. God would not allow anybody to approach His presence while in that state of existence under this situation. Had man eaten of the Tree of Life instead, he would yet today exist in fellowship with God without having been cast away and in need of redemption. We would have existed upon the principle of living by God's Eternal Life, Itself.

So, the two trees represent two ways of life. They speak of two principles upon which all people base their existences.

THE BARRIER

Since Cherubim were first presented to us in the Bible as guardians blocking man after man partook of the Tree of the Knowledge of Good and Evil, we must keep this association in mind when we come across them again. To summarize the thought, Cherubim stood as a barrier because man ingested the Knowledge of Good and Evil. A barrier exists so long as man has this principle of *lifestyle* driving his existence. This influences even his very approach to the things of God. Man brought about the need for the barrier since it was man's own fault that he ingested the Knowledge of Good and Evil. Hence, indirectly, the Knowledge of Good and Evil became a barrier to mankind which separated man from God. The Barrier of Knowledge.

"FORERUNNER" IMPLIES WE FOLLOW

Hebrews 6:19-20 lays forth the fact that Jesus is presently standing beyond a veil. He is there as forerunner.

Let us read it again.

Hebrews 6:19-20 Which hope we have as an anchor of the soul, both sure and stedfast, and which entereth into that

BARRIER OF KNOWLEDGE, PATHWAY OF LOVE

within the veil; **Whither the forerunner is for us entered**, *even Jesus, made an high priest for ever after the order of Melchisedec.*

Christ is past the veil. The same hope and faith we have today as believers is that which brings us in there as well. Since Christ is called a forerunner, we must realize that where He has entered is the same position into which we are intended to walk. We, like Jesus, must pass the veil.

In order to fully grasp the picture we read here in Hebrews, we must consider the Old Testament description of the veil that is mentioned in these verses. The writer directed our minds back to the veil noted in the Tabernacle and Temple that was situated in the Holy Place as a barrier to the entrance of the Holy of Holies. This symbolism of the veil relates a message.

Exodus 26:31 And thou shalt make a vail of blue, and purple, and scarlet, and fine twined linen of cunning work: with cherubims shall it be made:

The workers embroidered the image of the same Cherubim which served as a barrier to the Garden of Eden on the face of the veil. In this case they represented a barrier to the Holiest of Holies. Man's plight of alienation from the Garden of God was not yet solved in the days of the Temple. God, in effect, told man that he still could not approach the kind of fellowship with God that Adam once knew before his fall.

In effect, the barrier of knowledge was still standing in the days of the Old Testament!

However, in Hebrews, we read that we can pass the veil! Since Christ first passed the veil, and since He is forerunner, we too can now pass that veil. But it requires *a hope* that the writer of Hebrews mentioned.

We must ensure we have that faith. Let us not take for granted that all believers already possess this veil-breaching faith and hope, for we know that some have weak faith. Following the point of the writer of Hebrews will give us the benefit of knowing what it is that we must concentrate upon. We can perceive by reading Hebrews that it is a very important element of the Christian life.

We understand we must pass a veil. The means by which we can do this is by possessing a certain kind of faith and using it. This faith will take us past the Knowledge of Good and Evil – past the veil – past the Cherubim!

WHAT IS THE KNOWLEDGE OF GOOD AND EVIL?

Since it is one of the two principles of living, we must understand precisely what this principle involves in order for us to learn to avoid living by such a principle.

Well, one thing that the principle of the Knowledge of Good and Evil is not is Life. This tree of knowledge stood in opposition to the Tree of Life. Man could eat of Life, but not of the Knowledge of Good and Evil. Let us consider that the Life from the Tree of Life would have enabled Adam to live forever, had he eaten of its fruit. Therefore, it is not common life, but rather eternal Life. Eternal Life is not merely something which God possesses. It describes what God is. He is Life.

When God was manifest in the flesh as a man, He said:

> *John 14:6 ...I am the way, the truth, and the life: no man cometh unto the Father, but by me.*

Jesus is life.

Another thing which describes God's essence is LOVE.

> *1 John 4:8 He that loveth not knoweth not God; for God is love.*

He is *Life* and He is *Love*. Therefore, *Love* is *Life*. Life and Love are interlinked. We could say that there stood the Tree of *Love* and the Tree of the Knowledge of Good and Evil. In fact,

BARRIER OF KNOWLEDGE, PATHWAY OF LOVE

it becomes very clear that this is so as we begin to understand the two major principles of existence. All of humanity today is based upon one of these two principles. You are either basing your existence upon the principle of Life and love, or upon the principle of the Knowledge of Good and Evil.

Another word which goes well with love and life is *grace*. Grace is based upon *love*. This links us up with the Tree of Life. Grace is based upon love and not the Knowledge of Good and Evil because God looks down on an evil sinner and watches him repent of sins. God's love moves Him to *forgive* that sinner. Had not God possessed Grace, He would not *forgive*. To have no grace is to have no forgiveness. We need grace! We need Life! Not only that, but we must live by this principle and be able to forgive people as God forgave us.

Let us observe the characteristics of a person who does not know grace. When a person wrongs this individual, the thoughts that run through the mind are something like this: "He did me wrong! He did evil and not good! Therefore, I will not forgive him."

This person stands upon the basis of looking at everything from the perspective of the Knowledge of Good and Evil. In such a heart exists no forgiveness. All the person can see is whether there is a good act or an evil act in question.

One who possesses grace responds to a similar situation in this manner: "I will forgive him even if he did do evil, for God forgave me when I was wrong."

By comparing these two reactions let us notice that the former individual cannot see past the fault, and stands as a judge in the matter. One stops at the barrier of *knowledge*. Grace, on the other hand, *looks past the fault* and sees something deeper within the person. As Dottie Rambo sang, *"He looked beyond my fault and saw my need."* As God acts in grace towards humanity, the believer whose life is based upon the principle of Love and Life likewise sees past the *barrier of knowledge*.

Not Knowledge in General

Let me pause at this time to stress that I am not talking about *knowledge* in general. I am referring to the specific Knowledge of Good and Evil. I am not saying that education and the pursuit of human knowledge is to be avoided. Not at all. Too much of that absurd thinking has gone on amongst Christians for too long. It is the principle of lifestyle and existence which influences all our ways with one another and even with God. It's the Knowledge of Good and Evil that the Lord desires us to avoid. Such knowledge keeps us away from God in the Garden, and we must get it out of our lives!

> *Ephesians 3:16-19 That he would grant you, according to the riches of his glory, to be strengthened with might by his Spirit in the inner man; That Christ may dwell in your hearts by faith; that ye, being rooted and grounded in love, May be able to comprehend with all saints what is the breadth, and length, and depth, and height; And to know the love of Christ, which passeth knowledge, that ye might be filled with all the fulness of God.*

Paul's desire was that we pass the *barrier of knowledge* and enter into the vast expanse of God's fullness – the breadth, width, height and length. *Faith* causes Christ to live and dwell within our hearts. Recall that Hebrews spoke of hope, or faith, which moves us into a dimension that is said to be *past the veil*. Here we read that faith is linked to entering a domain that is wide, broad, high, and long – a domain in which we can comprehend with all saints a greater realm of spirituality in Christ. It is a place in which we know Christ's love. That love *passeth knowledge*! It passes the barrier!

We can apply this to many things. It looks beyond faults, and sees needs. It even takes us past the very barrier that mankind caused to stand between himself and God. It takes us into deep fellowship with God!

BARRIER OF KNOWLEDGE, PATHWAY OF LOVE

Lack of Grace and love puts us in the seats of judges. God will not allow us into the fellowship that stands past the barrier if we live by this false principle of life.

We must go past knowledge. That does not mean we relegate evil acts away as being unimportant issues. No. Evil is still evil and good is still good. Yet we must understand that, though we can still see evil and good in others, we must not stop there in our relationship with others, and judge them by that. We must see past that barrier and recognize something seen by God.

JUDGMENTAL SPIRITS

Some people are often so hard on others. Too many people give too little space for error in others. The smallest fault is exaggerated and dwelt upon by the critic and the judge, and it is cause for the poor victim to experience much harsh treatment.

The paradox is that the hard-hearted person is also hard on him/herself. Such people are in a most miserable state. They know what is right and wrong. They know good and evil, but dwelling on that aspect of existence alone will drive one mad. This is an imperfect world. The reason we sense the need for a "better life" is because Adam really did have that better life but fell from it, taking all the world with him. That ancient memory of a better life is within all of us in some latent form. If there never really was an *"Adam"*, and there was not a fall from grace, why is it that we look at life and instinctively believe it should be better? What gives us the awareness that things could be better? Why do we have a concept of *better*?

If things were always as they are now, then we should instinctively have adjusted to it, and never took a thought to see it any better.

The fact is that Adam did exist, Adam did fall and all humanity has fallen with him. Yet we cannot expect any better of this world for the time being. It is imperfect and will remain so until Jesus comes!

We cannot make ourselves better, that is for sure. How can fallen humanity lift fallen humanity out of a fallen state?

The perfectionist who bases existence on the Knowledge of Good and Evil, ever trying to rid the world and self of evil, will run in circles and circles, never accomplishing that end. One will always see fault, and always remain upset. What misery!

A world that is not perfect does not need perfectionists. It needs *love*.

Thank God that He does not base Himself upon the principle of the Knowledge of Good and Evil! If He did, nobody could ever be saved from sin since nobody would ever be forgiven. Everyone would get what they deserved, and none of us deserved Heaven.

The Knowledge of Good and Evil allows for no forgiveness.

BACKSLIDER'S PLIGHT

I saw many *backslide* away from the Christian life and walk back into the sinful lifestyles of the world. Many of them manifest a particular criticism of the Church. They slip into the principle of the Knowledge of Good and Evil and, like the very devil himself, accuse and accuse and accuse the brethren. The most notable element about the backslider is the judgmental, *unforgiving* attitude against the people of God.

Like Adam, they fall and blame their ills on somebody else!

> *Genesis 3:11-13 And he said, Who told thee that thou wast naked? Hast thou eaten of the tree, whereof I commanded thee that thou shouldest not eat? And the man said, The woman whom thou gavest to be with me, she gave me of the tree, and I did eat. And the LORD God said unto the woman, What is this that thou hast done? And the woman said, The serpent beguiled me, and I did eat.*

Adam and his wife blamed another for their own sin. Pass the buck!

BARRIER OF KNOWLEDGE, PATHWAY OF LOVE

KNOWLEDGE OF GOOD AND EVIL BARS US FROM GOD

We see how knowledge bars us from seeing the needs of others. More importantly, it also bars us from God, Himself. Those who base life upon the Knowledge of Good and Evil will never reach God! They will dwell on good and evil acts to such an extent that they believe their only chance of getting back to Him is to be as good as possible and never commit evil. They cannot see past the surface of the barrier of knowledge. They cannot see the inner root of the problem of SIN. Sin is a principle. It is the *factory* that produces the evil actions we call sins. *Sin* (singular), in this context, is not the same entity as *sins* (plural). *Sin* causes us to commit *sins*. If all that we are concerned with is whether something is categorized as good or evil, we will concentrate on stopping the evil activity and leave the root of the problem untouched. We will base our religion upon good works as the means *to take us to God*. But such an approach is based upon the Knowledge of Good and Evil, and it will ultimately *bar us from God*.

THE FUNDAMENTAL NEED FOR FORGIVENESS

Such people do not truly understand the need for forgiveness. They do not conceive the concept of asking God to *forgive* us. The reason this is so is because such an individual possesses no more than the idea that man must stop committing evil and instead commit good. Forgiveness only exists when there is a need to *overlook* error. I am not saying there is no need for repentance and asking forgiveness on the part of the sinner. The Bible clearly teaches us to repent and confess our sins, admitting we were wrong. However, the need to overlook error is required when error cannot be otherwise dealt with after we repent. Since we cannot help ourselves return to God by making ourselves behave *better*, God's love moved Him to resort to *forgiveness*.

Our good is never good enough for God, since it originates with humans who are imperfect, and God *is* perfect. His *Love*, though, moved Him to choose to forgive those who will admit their sin and accept God's provision of escape from sin through Christ's death. This renders people as justified, righteous, and fit to pass the barrier of knowledge, and return to fellowship with Him once again!

LAW LACKS GRACE

A police officer is not supposed to stop the violator, who is proven guilty of breaking the speed limit of a highway, and *forgive* that violator. The officer may *warn* the offender and let it go by for this time, but that is not really forgiveness.

A murderer may truly proclaim sorrow over his act of killing another person, but the judge will never *forgive* that person: "You are wrong, and you can be as sorry as you like, but you will still go to prison."

There is no way past the Knowledge of Good and Evil since there is no forgiveness involved in that principle of life. Forgiveness does not apply to this principle.

Since man has sin within himself, so long as it is there, man will never get to God without God's forgiveness. So we find two different aspects of the barrier of knowledge that will bar man from God.

1. A person will not allow oneself to approach God because their attempts to improve their actions and make themselves good will never satisfy God. The one who seeks perfection through self-righteousness will never find it. The instinct that makes us aware of our imperfection will keep us from ever daring to approach God.

2. God will not allow a person past the barrier because His word declares that approach to Himself is not of works lest any man should boast. Should God allow man to perfect oneself, which is impossible anyway, man would forever stand upon his

own efforts. Standing upon our own efforts would cause us to worship ourselves instead of God. God will not allow that.

IT HAD TO BE GRACE

The only course God could take in dealing with man's sin was to implement GRACE. By no other means could man return to God. Man had sin within himself and man could not remove it, himself.

Therefore, we understand how the Knowledge of Good and Evil stood as a barrier, but *love* made a *pathway* through the barrier! There is both the *Barrier of Knowledge* and the *Pathway of Love*.

Jesus went past the veil of the Knowledge of Good and Evil. He is our forerunner! We may pass the barrier also and experience the love that "passeth knowledge"!

ARK OF THE COVENANT: LIFE OVERRIDES KNOWLEDGE

Along with the veil of the Tabernacle, the Lord instructed Moses to build a chest to be called the Ark of the Covenant. Moses placed the tables of stone upon which was written the Ten Commandments, the rod of Aaron's priesthood, and the pot of manna that fed Israel in the wilderness in the Ark (Heb. 9:3-4).

Throughout Hebrews 9, the writer explained how the various articles of furniture symbolically spoke a message to the believer. The Ark is one of these symbolic articles of furniture.

(Should one ever find that Ark today and hope to find supernatural power, one would be disappointed. The Ark was used in the pre-Christian days of the Law of Moses, and it was God's presence upon that Ark that gave it power. But Christ came and did away with the Old Covenant rituals and symbols and brought the actual elements which the Old Testament items merely represented. Christ, Himself, is the *Ark* today!)

The tables of the commandments represent the Law of Moses. That Law was the Knowledge of Good and Evil. The law, itself, was not evil, but since man housed sin within him, man could not keep such a holy law (Romans 7:14). In other words, supplying the Knowledge of Good and Evil was not what man needed. Sin within man made it impossible for him to apply that knowledge and use it by making oneself line up to the good, and avoid the evil.

Within the Ark was the Knowledge of Good and Evil. But *covering* that chest was the Mercy Seat – a solid golden lid or cover which was placed over the open chest of the Ark. Upon this lid were the images of two Cherubim! And this Mercy Seat was to be splattered with the blood of the atonement sacrifice which was made every year in order to remove Israel's sins from them for another year.

That blood represented and foreshadowed the precious blood of Jesus Christ to be shed on the cross to remove man's sin, not for one year alone but, forever! (Ex. 25:10-19; Lev. 16:14; Rom. 5:11).

Blood was sprinkled on the Mercy Seat! Blood is representative of *Life*.

> *Leviticus 17:11 For the life of the flesh is in the blood: and I have given it to you upon the altar to make an atonement for your souls: for it is the blood that maketh an atonement for the soul.*

So, in seeing the blood sprinkled on the cover of the Ark that contained the law, we see a picture of the manner in which the principle of *Life* overrides the principle of the Knowledge of Good and Evil!

Love has *grace* for the failures which are proclaimed in a person's life by the Law.

BARRIER OF KNOWLEDGE, PATHWAY OF LOVE

GOD IS A FORGIVER

God does not want perfectionists in His church. He wants *forgivers.*

1 Corinthians 13:4-6 Charity suffereth long, and is kind; charity envieth not; charity vaunteth not itself, is not puffed up, Doth not behave itself unseemly, seeketh not her own, is not easily provoked, thinketh no evil; Rejoiceth not in iniquity, but rejoiceth in the truth;

1 Corinthians 13:7-13 Beareth all things, believeth all things, hopeth all things, endureth all things. Charity never faileth: but whether there be prophecies, they shall fail; whether there be tongues, they shall cease; whether there be knowledge, it shall vanish away. For we know in part, and we prophesy in part. But when that which is perfect is come, then that which is in part shall be done away. When I was a child, I spake as a child, I understood as a child, I thought as a child: but when I became a man, I put away childish things. For now we see through a glass, darkly; but then face to face: now I know in part; but then shall I know even as also I am known. And now abideth faith, hope, charity, these three; but the greatest of these is charity.

LOVE DOESN'T THINK THE WORST

Love, according to verse 7, hopes for the best! Have you ever noticed how critics approach a situation in which the full truth is not known and they tend to think the worst? For example, a promise was made by an individual to meet another at a certain time. The other person waits and waits, and never does meet the one who promised to come. The other person begins to imagine, not knowing what actually happened, and thinks that the person relegated the rendezvous to merely a waste of time and chose to not even bother with the meeting. Evil thoughts begin to formulate and soon a hatred exists which is based upon pure assumption. The worst possible scenario is thought.

This, of course, is extreme (although many have done this very thing!), but it shows my point. Why can we not think and hope for the best? Love *hopes* all things. Love covers a multitude of sins and overlooks faults. Love forgives. That is not to say that forgiveness is blind to faults. If that were so, then it would not even be love, for forgiveness only exists if there is a fault at hand. One who dwells upon love will always think for the best rather than think the worst.

> *Luke 7:47 Wherefore I say unto thee, Her sins, which are many, are forgiven; for she loved much: but to whom little is forgiven, the same loveth little.*

The harlot was forgiven of much sin. In turn, she manifested much love for Jesus. Let us learn a lesson. A true believer is not a nit-picker, but a forgiver!

The world is full of imperfect and damaged people. Therefore, the only Church that is going to successfully win this world is going to be a Church filled with forgivers. Think of what bad feelings would be averted if all believers based their Christianity upon life (which includes love) rather than the Knowledge of Good and Evil!

Failures do not remove you from God's love. That is the nature of love. It goes past knowledge.

People who are bound by the curse of the Knowledge of Good and Evil will commit an error and so condemn themselves that they walk away from God, not realizing He is ready to forgive them should they only ask! The power of condemnation is the Knowledge of Good and Evil. Since they base their lives upon the principle of knowledge, they do not conceive forgiveness properly. God is a God of grace.

Such people who thrive on the principle of knowledge must be delivered from that way of life by fellowshipping with believers who are forgivers. They need *safe* relationships where they will not be negatively criticized.

Love passeth knowledge.

So many believers mistakenly base their Christianity on the Knowledge of Good and Evil! It seems to be a natural instinct if we have not been taught otherwise. Such believers must learn the truth and be freed from the bondage of condemnation.

Basing our beliefs upon the Knowledge of Good and Evil will move us to doubt God's love for us, which is a contradiction since the meaning of love involves forgiveness. What a state into which the devil threw man! Not only did man fall into sin at the devil's temptation, but man ingested this cursed Knowledge of Good and Evil. This inbred principle of looking at life causes one to wrongfully feel that God hates us when we act sinfully, and in effect causes us to keep ourselves from repenting! If we do not repent, God cannot forgive us! Oh, how the world needs to know the truth. Many believers need to know this truth as well!

Love is a pathway that passes the barrier of Knowledge.

8

THE SIGNIFICANCE OF ZION AND THE CHURCH

There is one Old Testament passage that is quoted more times in the New Testament than any other. It is a Kingdom passage.

> *Psalms 110:1 A Psalm of David. The LORD said unto my Lord, Sit thou at my right hand, until I make thine enemies thy footstool.*

Jesus was said to have ascended to the Right Hand position when He ascended into glory (Mark 16:19).

The Right Hand throne is at Zion according to this Psalm.

> *Psalms 110:2 The LORD shall send the rod of thy strength **out of Zion**: rule thou in the midst of thine enemies.*

Jesus, Himself, quoted it as He asked the religious leaders how David's son, the Messiah, could be David's Lord (Matt. 22:42-45). Peter quoted it on the Day of Pentecost as cause for the speaking in other tongues that occurred that day (Acts 2:33). The first Christian Martyr, Stephen, even saw a vision of Christ at the right hand position of Kingdom power as he was dying (Acts 7:55-56). The Book of Hebrews quoted it in indication of Christ's greater position than any angel could hold (Heb 1:3, 13), as well as in association with His High Priesthood (Heb 8:1) and His sin-remitting single sacrifice (Heb. 10:12). This Right Hand enthronement of Jesus is even symbolically shown in the Book of Revelation (Rev. 22:1).

Surely the early Church knew what it was to understand the Kingdom of Heaven in their time. For something such as this to be quoted more than any other issue from the Old Testament, the early Church must have known powerful truths about the subject.

We need the inspiration and enlightenment of the Holy Ghost in order to truly appreciate what those early believers knew so well.

SPIRIT BAPTISM CAME DUE TO CHRIST'S RIGHT HAND ENTHRONEMENT

Peter received more revelation about Jesus and this Kingdom in just a few hours on the Day of Pentecost after he was first filled with the Spirit, than he had learned in over three years of following the Lord before the cross. Something absolutely revelatory occurred in his spirit when he was filled with the Baptism of the Holy Spirit. As thousands gathered outside the house of the upper room to learn what odd events occurred there in Jerusalem, Peter explained how the speaking with other tongues that everyone saw and heard that day was the result of Christ's attainment of the *right hand throne position.*

> *Acts 2:32-33 This Jesus hath God raised up, whereof we all are witnesses.* **Therefore being by the right hand of God exalted**, *and having received of the Father the promise of the Holy Ghost,* **he hath shed forth this, which ye now see and hear.**

What did he mean by the thought that Jesus was at the right hand of God? Are there at least two thrones in glory – one for the Father and at His right hand another for the Son? No. Jesus,

Himself, said that He actually sat down with His Father on His Father's throne.

> *Revelation 3:21 To him that overcometh will I grant to sit with me in my throne, even as I also overcame,* **and am set down with my Father in his throne.**

"Right hand" in this sense does not mean the right, physical side of someone. It is a term denoting *power*. Even today we use the term "right hand man" for the man of *power* in an organization.

God's *right hand* dashed in pieces the enemy of Israel when the Egyptians were drowned in the Red Sea (Ex. 15:6). Did that mean a giant right hand of God reached down from heaven into the earth and destroyed the armies in one fell swoop? No. It meant the *power of God* destroyed the armies by causing the Red Sea to drown them out.

How did Christ's seating at the right hand cause 120 people to speak with other tongues they never learned before?

> *Acts 2:33 Therefore being by the right hand of God exalted, and having received of the Father the promise of the Holy Ghost, he hath shed forth this, which ye now see and hear.*

Notice Peter made reference to the reception of the promise from the Father. Jesus said He had to leave the disciples and go to the Father so they could work greater accomplishments than even He, Himself, did.

> *John 14:12 Verily, verily, I say unto you, He that believeth on me, the works that I do shall he do also; and* **greater works than these shall he do; because I go unto my Father.**

Jesus claimed He had to go to the Father in order to have them receive the Comforter, the Holy Ghost.

THE SIGNIFICANCE OF ZION AND THE CHURCH

John 14:16 And I will pray the Father, and he shall give you another Comforter, that he may abide with you for ever;

John 14:26 But the Comforter, which is the Holy Ghost, whom the Father will send in my name, he shall teach you all things, and bring all things to your remembrance, whatsoever I have said unto you.

John 16:7 Nevertheless I tell you the truth; It is expedient for you that I go away: for if I go not away, the Comforter will not come unto you; but if I depart, I will send him unto you.

John 16:13 Howbeit when he, the Spirit of truth, is come, he will guide you into all truth: for he shall not speak of himself; but whatsoever he shall hear, that shall he speak: and he will shew you things to come.

Luke 24:49 And, behold, I send the promise of my Father upon you: but tarry ye in the city of Jerusalem, until ye be endued with power from on high.

The reception of the promise of the Father was the endowment of the Gift of the Holy Spirit. The disciples did indeed tarry in Jerusalem and received the power of the Holy Ghost which caused them to speak with other tongues (Acts 2:1-4). Peter explained it was all because Jesus had gone to the *Right Hand Throne*. So, the Right Hand is not beside God's Throne, but rather is God's throne itself. It is the Right Hand Throne. As a throne is a place of power, the term "right hand" denotes power. So it is a Right Hand Throne. Peter said this experience of speaking in tongues came as the result of Jesus having gone to the Father, or in other words, sat down with the Father at the Right Hand throne position. There is only One Throne. God and the Lamb are both seated together in this Throne (Rev. 22:1). Just as a River poured forth from the throne of God and the Lamb in Rev. 22:1, Peter said the Spirit was *shed forth* because Jesus sat at the Right Hand (Acts 2:33).

What Peter experienced as he spoke words about Jesus at that Right Hand throne was Kingdom Revelation! He received direct revelation of how Christ's enthronement caused what everyone witnessed that day, due to the inspiration of the Spirit. He went into quite an elaborate explanation of how the prophecies of David had come to pass before everyone's eyes.

WHAT IS THE RIGHT HAND THRONE ALL ABOUT?

The concept of the "right hand" throne of God was foretold several times in the Prophets and Psalms. David began writing about it ever since the Lord spoke to him of a Kingdom in which his Son would rule. This Son's throne would never be taken from him. God told David that his family dynasty would continue forever.

> *2 Samuel 7:12-16 And when thy days be fulfilled, and thou shalt sleep with thy fathers, I will set up thy seed after thee, which shall proceed out of thy bowels, and I will establish his kingdom. He shall build an house for my name, and I will stablish the throne of his kingdom for ever. I will be his father, and he shall be my son. If he commit iniquity, I will chasten him with the rod of men, and with the stripes of the children of men: But my mercy shall not depart away from him, as I took it from Saul, whom I put away before thee. And thine house and thy kingdom shall be established for ever before thee: thy throne shall be established for ever.*

Solomon literally fulfilled this prophecy, as son of David. He even experienced mercy after his sins to see the kingdom removed in his successor's time and not his own. But the true and greater fulfillment of this was to be experienced in the Greater Son of David, Jesus Christ (Matt. 1:1). Christ would not sin,

THE SIGNIFICANCE OF ZION AND THE CHURCH

though, and would literally remain seated on the throne forever having resurrected to sit there and never die again in immortality! Not only did the experiences of Solomon find greater and more perfect fulfillment in Jesus Christ, even the events David himself experienced were foreshadows of Christ's dominion. Peter actually had to point out that though one might think David referred to himself in a prophetic Psalm about not being left in the grave to see corruption (Psalm 16:10), David prophesied of Christ's resurrection (Acts 2:27-31). David's body was still in the grave. How could that have spoken of him? So we see precedent for looking at David and seeing messages about Jesus Christ.

DAVID TAKES ZION

With this in mind, note that the Bible recounts the time when David first took Jerusalem, formerly named Jebusi (also Jebus), and conquered the castle of Zion in that city. David was just anointed the third time as King, but this time by all of Israel. Formerly, Samuel anointed him as a boy (1 Samuel 16:13), then Judah anointed him over their kingdom (2 Samuel 2:4), but now all the tribes of Israel recognized him as King (2 Samuel 5:3). The first thing he did was proceed to conquer all of Jerusalem. Zion was a stronghold that Israel could never acquire beforehand since the days of Joshua when they first claimed possession of the Promised Land and took Jerusalem. In fact, the people of Jebusi mocked David's ability to take the stronghold as though he could not even overcome the lame and blind. These cripples may have been actually used in mockery to stand as guards of Zion while David attempted to conquer it. David did in fact conquer Zion (2 Samuel 5:6-7) and called it the City of David (2 Samuel 5:9).

After time, the Philistines heard about David's possession of Zion when all of Israel accepted him as King, and joined forces with other strong nations to depose him.

> *2 Samuel 5:17 But when the Philistines heard that they had anointed David king over Israel, all the Philistines came up to seek David; and David heard of it, and went down to the hold.*

The King asked the Lord if he should go forth and fight, lest David miss God's will and fail. David learned to rely upon the leading of the Lord in every step he made. God told him to fight for he would doubtlessly be victor (2 Samuel 5:19).

Needless to say, David won an overwhelming victory, and actually wrote about it in the **Second Psalm**. Read how David was given Zion, and yet the heathens raged and sought to dethrone and remove him from there. Note, also, where God was said to inform him that He set David on Zion, and that meant God would grant him any victory he requested.

> *Psalms 2:1-6 Why do the heathen rage, and the people imagine a vain thing? The kings of the earth set themselves, and the rulers take counsel together, against the LORD, and against his anointed, saying, Let us break their bands asunder, and cast away their cords from us. (4) He that sitteth in the heavens shall laugh: the Lord shall have them in derision. Then shall he speak unto them in his wrath, and vex them in his sore displeasure. Yet have I set my king upon my holy hill of Zion.*

Just as the book of 2 Samuel recounted how David took Zion and the Philistines sought to dethrone him, we read in Psalm 2 of the heathen raging despite the fact God set David on Zion. We even read of the Lord laughing at the heathen in Psalm 2 just as they initially laughed and mocked David's attempt to conquer them in 2 Samuel.

THE SIGNIFICANCE OF ZION AND THE CHURCH

EARLY CHURCH RECOGNIZED THAT ZION REFERRED TO THEM

What is so interesting about this Psalm is that it was quoted by the early church in the book of Acts after Peter and John healed a crippled man at the Temple, and were persecuted by the religious leaders of the city.

> *Acts 3:6-8 Then Peter said, Silver and gold have I none; but such as I have give I thee: In the name of Jesus Christ of Nazareth rise up and walk. And he took him by the right hand, and lifted him up: and immediately his feet and ankle bones received strength. And he leaping up stood, and walked, and entered with them into the Temple, walking, and leaping, and praising God.*

> *Acts 3:16 And his name through faith in his name hath made this man strong, whom ye see and know: yea, the faith which is by him hath given him this perfect soundness in the presence of you all.*

> *Acts 4:1-3 And as they spake unto the people, the priests, and the captain of the Temple, and the Sadducees, came upon them, Being grieved that they taught the people, and preached through Jesus the resurrection from the dead. And they laid hands on them, and put them in hold unto the next day: for it was now eventide.*

> *Acts 4:18 And they called them, and commanded them not to speak at all nor teach in the name of Jesus.*

They were in the same city David wrote about, Jerusalem. But there was more than that which they had in common with the events mentioned in the Second Psalm. As soon as the church heard Peter and John's report of being commanded to not preach nor speak again in the name of Jesus, they cried out the words of the Second Psalm.

> *Acts 4:24-25 And when they heard that, they lifted up their voice to God with one accord, and said, Lord, thou art God, which hast made heaven, and earth, and the sea, and all that in them is: Who by the mouth of thy servant David hast said, Why did the heathen rage, and the people imagine vain things?*

They interpreted those words and applied them to their situation by saying the heathen who raged were actually the kings of the earth *in their day*.

> *Acts 4:26-27 The kings of the earth stood up, and the rulers were gathered together against the Lord, and against his Christ. For of a truth against thy holy child Jesus, whom thou hast anointed, both Herod, and Pontius Pilate, with the Gentiles, and the people of Israel, were gathered together,*

A mighty revelation came into their spirits! Just as David had ascended to Zion and conquered it, making it his city and the place of his throne, Jesus Christ resurrected from the grave and ascended into glory to sit at the right hand position of the throne. The early Church knew that the setting of David on Zion, calling David God's "son" who was in a sense *"begotten"* that day, spoke of Jesus Christ's resurrection!

> *Acts 13:33 God hath fulfilled the same unto us their children, in that he hath raised up Jesus again; as it is also written in the second psalm, Thou art my Son, this day have I begotten thee.*

> *Psalms 2:6-7 Yet have I set my king upon my holy hill of Zion. I will declare the decree: the LORD hath said unto me, Thou art my Son; this day have I begotten thee.*

When the Philistines heard of this, they "raged" and imagined "vain things". They set forth to dethrone David, but David prayed just as *the church prayed when an assault was threatened against Jesus*. It was as though the church saw David as foreshadowing Jesus Who took the *right hand throne* of God, and the Philistines standing in the place of the priests, captain of the Temple and the Sadducees who set forth to dethrone Jesus. His name was preached throughout all Jerusalem!

The manner in which the Church *conquered* this "Philistine" Sadducaean threat, as David maintained Zion, was through the empowerment of the Holy Ghost. The Spirit of God caused them to *continue to speak that name with boldness* despite the threat for them to stop.

> *Acts 4:31 And when they had prayed, the place was shaken where they were assembled together; and they were all filled with the Holy Ghost,* **and they spake the word of God with boldness.**

AN EXAMPLE OF APPLYING KINGDOM TRUTH TO OUR BATTLES

This shows us something very enlightening for us as Christians! The early church took prophecies of the Kingdom position of Jesus Christ and applied it to themselves and their day. They knew they were in that Kingdom and were going forth to conquer in Jesus' Name as David fought for Zion and maintained it. Jesus went to the true Zion and sat on the throne of the Right Hand. This Kingdom of His Name must continue to be proclaimed. It was their duty to see it done. They learned that David's exploits for Zion were prophetic pictures for the Church of the living God to carry out the greater fulfillment in their day.

BE KINGDOM-MINDED

Think of the trials and troubles we have in our lives today as Christians. We need to learn to be so Kingdom-minded that we likewise think of our situations in light of Christ's enthronement. This allows us to respond accordingly in the power of that Kingdom and see victory! This is what the early Church did.

What comes to our minds when we face trials? When we have need of healing or a financial miracle. What do we do? Rather than fret and think of how impossible a situation might be in which we find ourselves, we need to remember that Jesus is on the throne. We are born into His Kingdom. Because He is on that throne, and all power in Heaven and Earth is His, we can claim a miracle to meet our needs!

As surely as God set David on Zion and would answer David's needs, what we pray for will come to pass.

When persecution hit the early believers, they realized they did not have to back down, for Christ is King on the throne at the Right Hand. If David was set there to stay, and God would give him any victory he requested because of it, surely we can go forth in Kingdom power and defeat our enemies. We must realize, though, that our enemies are not so much actual people, but principalities and powers in high places (Eph. 6:12). This is the reason the Church did not physically battle the Sadducees and other religious leaders with swords and spears. They conquered demonic powers through the inspiration of boldness by the Holy Spirit. When fear gripped their hearts, it may have been inspired by the Sadducees, but it was a spirit of fear from the devil. The empowerment of the Holy Ghost to speak the Name of Jesus with boldness was how they defeated those "Philistines".

Go forth in the power of the Holy Spirit! Realize Jesus is on the Right Hand throne of this Kingdom into which we've been born. Live and act this Christian life with a Kingdom consciousness that Christ is presently King of Kings and Lord of Lords. We have already come to Zion!

THE SIGNIFICANCE OF ZION AND THE CHURCH

> *Hebrews 12:22-23 But ye are come unto mount Sion, and unto the city of the living God, the heavenly Jerusalem, and to an innumerable company of angels, To the general assembly and church of the firstborn, which are written in heaven, and to God the Judge of all, and to the spirits of just men made perfect,*

WHO DARES TO AFFLICT THE KINGDOM PEOPLE?

The Second Psalm continues to describe the power the early church came to learn was at their disposal. Notice in this Psalm the promise to us to ask what we have need of and see an enemy against us defeated. Then watch how the Psalm ends with words of warning to those who would dare fight Christ's people in His Kingdom.

> *Psalms 2:8-12 Ask of me, and I shall give thee the heathen for thine inheritance, and the uttermost parts of the earth for thy possession. Thou shalt break them with a rod of iron; thou shalt dash them in pieces like a potter's vessel. Be wise now therefore, O ye kings: be instructed, ye judges of the earth. Serve the LORD with fear, and rejoice with trembling. Kiss the Son, lest he be angry, and ye perish from the way, when his wrath is kindled but a little. Blessed are all they that put their trust in him.*

The early church preached the name of Jesus and saw thousands of souls won into the Kingdom. The gospel eventually reached the Gentile world in Acts 10, and today we know salvation as Gentiles who have been born into this glorious Kingdom of Zion!

Let's go forth in the faith the early church had, and in revelation of Kingdom Living.

Romans 8:34 Who is he that condemneth? It is Christ that died, yea rather, that is risen again, who is even at the right hand of God, who also maketh intercession for us.

9

THE REVELATION OF THE ROCK

> *Matthew 16:13-20 When Jesus came into the coasts of Caesarea Philippi, he asked his disciples, saying, Whom do men say that I the Son of man am? And they said, Some say that thou art John the Baptist: some, Elias; and others, Jeremias, or one of the prophets. He saith unto them, But whom say ye that I am? And Simon Peter answered and said, Thou art the Christ, the Son of the living God. And Jesus answered and said unto him, Blessed art thou, Simon Barjona: for flesh and blood hath not revealed it unto thee, but my Father which is in heaven. And I say also unto thee, That thou art Peter, and upon this rock I will build my church; and the gates of hell shall not prevail against it. And I will give unto thee the keys of the kingdom of heaven: and whatsoever thou shalt bind on earth shall be bound in heaven: and whatsoever thou shalt loose on earth shall be loosed in heaven. Then charged he his disciples that they should tell no man that he was Jesus the Christ.*

The disciples came to a very crucial and significant point in their walks with Jesus. One of them received a direct revelation from the Father. Peter realized who Jesus was! After Jesus saw that the Father revealed His identity to Peter, then Jesus said, "…and I say also unto thee…"

Jesus had *an additional revelation* for Peter to receive. We see a picture of two distinct revelations, the second of which would not be given unless the first one was received. That is what thrilled Jesus so much. This secondary revelation dealt more specifically with Kingdom Living. It would render power and authority in the Kingdom to Peter.

The Lord said His church would be built like a house on the Rock. The gates of "hell", or the grave (Hades), would not prevail against it. As He continued to speak, more of what He actually meant came to the surface. However, notice that after Jesus commented on Peter's revelation from the Father, we read none of the disciples were allowed to rob others of that same experience of receiving revelation. Jesus told them to tell no man that He was the Christ. It seems Jesus meant for everyone else to likewise hear the Father speak to them as much as Peter received the revelation from the Father.

> *Matthew 16:20 Then charged he his disciples that they should tell no man that he was Jesus the Christ.*

That was the same thing Peter learned in revelation from the Father. Then Jesus began to speak some words He never revealed to them before.

> *Matthew 16:21-22 From that time forth began Jesus to shew unto his disciples, how that he must go unto Jerusalem, and suffer many things of the elders and chief priests and scribes, and be killed, and be raised again the third day. Then Peter took him, and began to rebuke him, saying, Be it far from thee, Lord: this shall not be unto thee.*

The words "from that time forth" distinguish that precise point in their walks with Him when Peter got a direct revelation from the Father about Jesus' identity. We find that, of all people, Peter actually resisted this second revelation! The very man who just received insight from the *Father* rejected the additional revelation from the *Son*. Peter did not like the information that Christ must suffer, die, and rise again. In that familiar, old, self-preserving style, Peter only heard about the suffering and the dying and missed the wonderful news of *resurrection*.

Recall that Jesus spoke of building His Church on the Rock. What Rock? The epistles inform us.

> *1 Corinthians 3:11 For other foundation can no man lay than that is laid, which is Jesus Christ.*

Some think the Rock is Peter, but Peter himself said it was Someone greater:

> *1 Peter 2:6-7 Wherefore also it is contained in the scripture, Behold, I lay in Sion a chief corner stone, elect, precious: and he that believeth on him shall not be confounded. Unto you therefore which believe he is precious: but unto them which be disobedient, the stone which the builders disallowed, the same is made the head of the corner,*

Of course we know the Rock is Christ. There is a vital relationship between the Church and the Rock upon which the Church is built. Any house is only as stable as the foundation upon which it stands. A house on sand falls when storms afflict it and a house on rock stands. In other words, the foundation's withstanding ability affects the house upon which it is built. The house is not its own stabilizing factor. The foundation is. A house is no better than its foundation.

"HELL" AS THE GRAVE

When the Lord spoke about the church on the Rock, He actually provided them with a revelation of His Bride coming into a *special union* with Him. That union would cause the Church to share His characteristics and qualities. To speak of the Church on the Rock, coupled with the idea that the gates of hell (the grave) would not overcome the Church, we see a note of the overcoming power of *resurrection*.

Translated from the Greek word "Gehenna", the term "hell" speaks of a place of fire, suffering and torment. But when "hell" is translated the Greek word "Hades," as in this case, it means something quite different. For this reason we are not always intended to think of fiery torment whenever we read the word "hell" in the Bible. It is necessary to research which Greek word was used to translate the English word "hell" in our Bibles in any given instance. This will help us not confuse the very real place of fire and torment with something else God is trying to explain to us.

"Hades" means "the grave" or "place of the dead." The place of the dead can involve the fires of hell, for sure, but sometimes the context is only speaking of the grave. So, when Jesus said that the gates of *the grave* would not prevail against the church built on the Rock, He was telling us that *resurrection from the dead* – from the grave – was involved in the Church's position on the Rock. How can the grave's gates not prevail against us, or hold us back, unless the concept of resurrection is implied? That is the reason Jesus continued to speak of suffering, dying, and rising from the dead afterwards. He spoke an encouraging word of the grave not holding us back and then spoke of His resurrection from the grave.

Had Peter grasped the words of Jesus correctly, he wouldn't have begged Jesus to forget about dying. He wouldn't have worried about his own neck in facing death due to following Jesus. Instead, he would have realized that, just as the Rock's stability is shared by the house built on top of it, Christ's own resurrection power is shared by the members of the Church who are built upon Him. The gates of the grave would not prevail against the Church!

When you know that Jesus has power over death in resurrection glory, and you are *built* on Him, so to speak, then you also share that power. That power is called "resurrection" from death.

THE REVELATION OF THE ROCK

The gospel songwriter wrote, *"Ain't no grave gonna hold my body down!"* Why? It is because we're in the Church that is built upon the Rock Jesus who has resurrected from the grave. We share that resurrection power with Him, like a house shares the foundation's stability.

> *Matthew 16:23 But he turned, and said unto Peter, Get thee behind me, Satan: thou art an offence unto me: for thou savourest not the things that be of God, but those that be of men.*

A MATTER OF IDENTITIES

After Jesus saw Peter recognize His identity by the revelation of the Father, He told Peter, "Thou art Peter. And upon this rock will I build my church." In other words, after Peter learned *Christ's identity*, he was then to learn something about *his own personal identity in Christ!* He would learn that, as much as a house on a Rock shares that Rock's unmoveable power, Peter would henceforth consider himself *one with the Son* and as immoveable, even by death, as Jesus was.

But when Peter refused to accept that revelation, the Lord said, "Get thee behind me, satan!" He changed His thought of *Peter's identity* and identified him as satan! Can we see how *identity* is the entire point here?

Peter was then an offence to Jesus. This idea of *offence* is a very vital one.

Recall that when Peter spoke of Jesus as a Rock in his own epistle, he called Him the Cornerstone upon which the church is built. He also explained that Jesus is a *Rock of offence* to those who are disobedient at His Word. Peter actually became an *offence*, himself, to the One who is an *offence* to the disobedient. Peter stumbled at the Word.

When the Rock is an offence to you, *you likewise* become an offence. But when you are in compliance with the Rock, you are a complement to it and it is a complement to you!

Peter resisted the "things that be of God." He resisted the need for death so that resurrection would follow. Just as Jesus compared how His resurrection power against the grave is shared by the church that is built upon Him, Jesus spoke of how His disciples must likewise share His coming experience of taking up a cross. He continued, saying...

> *Matthew 16:24-26 Then said Jesus unto his disciples, If any man will come after me, let him deny himself, and take up his cross, and follow me. For whosoever will save his life shall lose it: and whosoever will lose his life for my sake shall find it. For what is a man profited, if he shall gain the whole world, and lose his own soul? or what shall a man give in exchange for his soul?*

Believer, we must follow Jesus. Peter knew that, and that is why He told Jesus to forget about going to Jerusalem, suffering, and dying. Peter realized death was going to be his own experience should he continue to hang around this kind of Lord. However, Jesus pierced through Peter's false concern for Him, recognized Peter was actually concerned over his own neck, and stated plainly that they all must indeed take up their crosses and follow Him. They must deny themselves.

IF YOU DON'T TASTE DEATH NOW, YOU WILL LATER

In fact, Jesus said that some of them who would disobey Him may choose to *not taste death by taking up their crosses at that time*. That is their choice. But they had to know that they *would taste it later* when He would come in destruction. He spoke of the impending doom upon Jerusalem that would occur in AD70!

> *Matthew 16:27-28 For the Son of man shall come in the glory of his Father with his angels; and then he shall reward every man according to his works. Verily I say unto you,*

THE REVELATION OF THE ROCK

There be some standing here, which shall not taste of death, till they see the Son of man coming in his kingdom.

Think of it. Jesus just spoke of dying, and encouraged His followers to take up their crosses and die to themselves as well. Then He said some of them would not taste death. He informed them that He knew *there would be those who would choose to forget about denying themselves.* But whether we accept death now, or put it off for later, death is going to come one way or another. Jesus only showed them that death-to-self now would award one an eternal form of life.

This taste of death at Christ's coming did not refer to the yet future coming of Jesus that we anticipate even today. This spoke of the time when those people were still alive and faced a terrible coming of destruction in their lifetimes. It happened to be the coming of Christ in the power of His Kingdom. The message is: Those who accept the spiritual death of taking up their crosses today will experience a resurrection later. This spiritual death will not be permanent death. If, on the other hand, His disciples would not taste death (by the cross of self-denial), they would taste it when destruction would come during their lifetimes, which happened to occur in AD70. There would be no resurrection from that death!

In effect, Jesus claimed, "Some of you hearing me now will not deny yourselves and die spiritually. But I warn you that you will die later in a death from which you cannot get your life back again! Should you be willing to die now, you shall experience a resurrection due to a power you will share because of your union to Me."

This destruction that awaited those who refused to follow Him was precisely what Jesus referred to a few chapters later in Matthew's Gospel. Look particularly at the term *"cometh."* This is about a coming of the Lord.

> *Matthew 21:40-45* **When the lord therefore of the vineyard cometh**, *what will he do unto those husbandmen? They say unto him, He will miserably destroy those wicked men, and will let out his vineyard unto other husbandmen, which shall render him the fruits in their seasons. Jesus saith unto them, Did ye never read in the scriptures, The stone which the builders rejected, the same is become the head of the corner: this is the Lord's doing, and it is marvellous in our eyes? Therefore say I unto you, The kingdom of God shall be taken from you, and given to a nation bringing forth the fruits thereof. (44) And whosoever shall fall on this stone shall be broken: but on whomsoever it shall fall, it will grind him to powder. And when the chief priests and Pharisees had heard his parables, they perceived that he spake of them.*

Notice that all these words revolve around the mention of the *Kingdom*. Here we read that the Lord comes, and the Rock is *a stone of destruction*. The Pharisees knew that Jesus spoke directly about this as something to happen in their lifetimes to them.

One lesson to learn here is that some references to Christ's *coming* do not refer to the future coming that we all continue to anticipate and await. Some references spoke of a *coming* that occurred 2,000 years ago in the destruction against Jerusalem in the first century!

YOU MIGHT KNOW JESUS, BUT DOES JESUS KNOW YOU?

Keeping in mind the words about the Rock, and the concept of *knowing* someone's *identity*, let us read these passages…

> *Matthew 7:21-24* **Not every one that saith unto me, Lord, Lord**, *shall enter into the* **kingdom of heaven**; *but he that doeth the will of my Father which is in heaven. Many will say to me in that day,* **Lord, Lord**, *have we not prophesied in thy name? and in thy name have cast out devils?*

THE REVELATION OF THE ROCK

and in thy name done many wonderful works? And then will I profess unto them, **I never knew you:** *depart from me, ye that work iniquity. Therefore whosoever heareth these sayings of mine, and doeth them, I will liken him unto* **a wise man, which built his house upon a rock:**

Notice that the people in Christ's account had a revelation of His identity since they called Him "Lord." No man can call Jesus Lord but by the Spirit's revelation (1 Cor. 12:3). But when Jesus referred to them as *people whom He did not know*, and told them to depart since they were workers of iniquity, He explained they were *those who do not hear those sayings of His*.

They got a revelation from the Father, since they knew He was Lord. But when Jesus said, "And I say also unto you," they did not get this second revelation from the Son. Verse 24 noted that only those who hear *His sayings* and obey them are able to enter the Kingdom and *build a house on the Rock*.

Can you see how Matthew 16 and Peter's revelation of Jesus' identity corresponded to Matthew 7? People know Jesus' identity, but He does not recognize their identity since they refuse to hear His words. This is a powerful revelation! It is not enough to know who Jesus is. We must also know what He is saying to us! Jesus said elsewhere, "Why call me Lord, and not do the things I say?" (Luke 6:46).

Many who believe in Jesus may not necessarily be on the Rock. This might sound strange, since we often consider those on the Rock to be all believers by default. But consider something. Many may have a revelation of Jesus' identity, but their own identities are not so much known by Jesus *since they did not receive the further revelation regarding the Kingdom and the Rock*. Like Peter, they live in fear lacking a faith that comes from receiving a revelation of the Rock. They cannot trust God for victory over seemingly impossible situations. Peter knew who Jesus was, but was so fearful of death that he refused to accept Christ's further revelation, and it moved Jesus to refer to him as satan! Peter learned Christ's identity by the Father's revelation, and Jesus then informed Peter of his identity in Christ. "Thou art Peter, and upon this rock I will build my church." We need to learn who we are in Christ. But when Peter missed the revelation, Jesus called Peter by the name "satan." Peter missed the revelation of his own identity, and Jesus said he was acting like the devil. We need to learn who we are in Christ so that we can proceed to act upon it.

People will likewise know that Jesus is "Lord," but Jesus will tell them that *He never knew them!* In fact, Christ will say to them that *they are workers of iniquity* just as he called Peter, *"satan."*

SELF-DENIAL AWARDS RESURRECTION POWER

The reason the gates of the grave cannot prevail against the Church on the Rock is because the death of self-denial and following Jesus will result in resurrection! We cannot break through the gates of the grave in resurrection power if we refuse to taste death through taking up our crosses now.

I propose this resurrection from the dead is not just referring to rising from *physical* death. That is certainly involved. But there is also the thought that resurrection power of God's anointing comes upon us due to our willingness to experience self-denial. This is really a *death* to self. Sickness is a work of the same spirit of death. God's anointing can heal sickness and thereby overcome that form of death. Resurrection power is actually working when we see healings and miracles that affect a person's very health!

FRUITLESS AND FALSE PROPHETS

In Matthew 7, Jesus identified people as "workers of iniquity," even though they correctly understood His identity. What was He trying to say? The message is clear – these people did not *deny themselves*. This self-denial was explained in Matthew 16. They refused that further, secondary revelation.

THE REVELATION OF THE ROCK

People can know who Jesus is and yet still be referred to as workers of iniquity. It's not enough to know Jesus is Lord. Take the teachings of Matthew 16 and apply them to Matthew 7. When we take up our crosses and deny ourselves, we are killing out that power that causes us to commit *iniquity*. That is what the cross does. This is such an important step to take after our acceptance of Jesus as Lord. That is the reason people called Jesus "Lord," and he called them "*workers of iniquity*," just as Peter knew He was God's Son and Jesus called him "satan." Likewise, if we don't deny ourselves and take up our crosses, we are believers who cannot help but live as workers of iniquity. If the flesh is not crucified and denied in our lives, we cannot avoid committing works of the flesh.

Jesus explained all of this after having spoken about fruit and false prophets in Matthew 7. Let's go back a few verses before Jesus spoke of "workers of iniquity," and see what he was talking about.

> *Matthew 7:15-16 Beware of false prophets, which come to you in sheep's clothing, but inwardly they are ravening wolves. Ye shall know them by their fruits. Do men gather grapes of thorns, or figs of thistles?*

This is enlightening. Jesus spoke of false prophets and wolves in sheep's clothing. Then He immediately raised the topic of entering His Kingdom. People might know that Jesus is "Lord" and be able to perform miracles, but they do not obey the words Jesus spoke.

Let's put it altogether now and get the full picture. When he referred to false prophets, He did not necessarily talk about people from other religions, but rather those amongst God's people (after all, they're clothed in *sheep's clothing*). Such people who refuse to follow all of Christ's words, are people who do not deny themselves. The pattern in Matthew 7 and Matthew 16 is identical! People received the Father's revelation of Jesus' identity, but in both cases refused to accept the revelation and teachings from the Son.

> *Matthew 16:16-17* *And Simon Peter answered and said,* **Thou art the Christ, the Son of the living God.** *And Jesus answered and said unto him, Blessed art thou, Simon Barjona:* **for flesh and blood hath not revealed it unto thee, but my Father which is in heaven.**

> *Matthew 7:21* *Not* **every one that saith unto me, Lord, Lord,** *shall enter into the kingdom of heaven; but he that doeth* **the will of my Father** *which is in heaven.*

THE FATHER'S REVELATION IMPLIES THE FATHER'S WILL

It is marvelous to see that in both passages the Father is mentioned. In Matthew 16, Jesus said the Father revealed to Peter the identity of Christ. In Matthew 7, "the will of my Father" is mentioned. It is one thing to receive revelation from the Father, but then there is the will of the Father. The will of the Father is intimately connected to the revelation of the Father. When the Father reveals the identity of Jesus as Lord, He is implying something to a person. If Jesus is Lord, then the will of the Father is for us to obey this Lord. The entire point of recognizing Jesus as Lord is to recognize His Lordship over us. This implies there is a discovery that He will speak things we must obey.

In Luke's Gospel, the same teaching of the house on the Rock involves these very pertinent words:

> *Luke 6:46* *And why call ye me, Lord, Lord, and do not the things which I say?*

THE REVELATION OF THE ROCK

In both chapters we then see parallel thoughts concerning our need to hear what the *Lord* Jesus has to say, and obey Him.

Matthew 16:18 And I say also unto thee, ...

Matthew 7:24 Therefore **whosoever heareth these sayings of mine, and doeth them***, I will liken him unto a wise man, which built his house upon a rock:*

Jesus noted our need to obey His words after we recognize Who He is.

STOPPING WORKS OF INIQUITY

Many people accept the Father's revelation of Christ's identity, and refuse to accept and obey the Son's revelation of self-denial. Such people are unable to stop the power in their flesh that causes them to commit works of the flesh. They correctly profess and praise Jesus as the Lord, but they are not doing the will of the Father. The will of the Father is self-explanatory once the revelation from the Father is given. Why would the Father want us to know that Jesus is the Christ, the Son of the living God, and our Lord, if the Father did not want us to hear the Son and *obey Him*? Since Christ's words deal with denial of flesh and self, commanding us to deny them, we will remain workers of iniquity when we do not accept the revelation from the Son.

Jesus spoke of *false prophets* just before He mentioned the picture of people calling Jesus "Lord." This label was never used in the Bible to describe people with entirely aberrant and false religions. We loosely use that term to identify anyone who does not believe Jesus Christ is Lord and instead honours some other pagan deity. The scriptures, however, only use that title in reference to God's own people who stray into error. A person from an entirely false religion is rather called a heathen in Scripture. During Old Testament times, "False prophets" were those from Israel who veered off into disobedience to God. A proponent of another religion was not termed a "false prophet" although we know they were false. They were simply called pagans or heathens. In the New Testament they are people who know the truth and have either departed from it, or refused to follow it fully, while still calling themselves "Christians." They stopped with the Father's revelation of Jesus' identity, and refused to take up their crosses to deny themselves.

THE ROCK, INIQUITY AND KNOWING JESUS

When Paul spoke of "fruit of the Spirit" and "works of the flesh" in Galatians 5, he also said something that goes right along with this entire concept.

> *Galatians 5:24 And they that are Christ's have crucified the flesh with the affections and lusts.*

Notice we read about crucifixion amongst *believers*. Taking up our crosses to deny ourselves will remove the *works of iniquity* – or works of the flesh – from our lives because our flesh is crucified *along with its lusts*.

Paul said something else to Timothy in a chapter about a solid *foundation* and associated it with those who taught that the *resurrection* will never happen. (As we read, keep in mind that Jesus said those who obey His words and taste the death of *self-denial* will *resurrect* and find their lives again).

> *2 Timothy 2:18-19 Who concerning the truth have erred, saying that the **resurrection** is past already; and overthrow the faith of some. Nevertheless the **foundation** of God standeth **sure**, having this seal,* **The Lord knoweth them that are his. And, Let every one that nameth the name of Christ depart from iniquity.**

This is amazing! *Resurrection* is directly connected to the *foundation* of the Church, just as Jesus implied when He spoke of the

THE REVELATION OF THE ROCK

Church on the Rock against whom the gates of the grave cannot prevail!

As Christ's words in Matthew 7 concerned building a house on the rock, Paul wrote to Timothy about a *foundation/Rock*.

As Jesus spoke of not knowing certain believers, Paul wrote "The Lord **knoweth** them that are his."

As Jesus spoke of people *departing* from Him since they were "workers of *iniquity*", Paul wrote those who name Christ (know His identity) must **depart** from *iniquity* (or, receive and obey the further revelation of self-denial).

All three points of a Rock foundation, knowing Jesus, and the issue of iniquity are seen in these two chapters. Putting Matthew 7 together with 2 Timothy 2, we get this overall understanding:

- If you are on the Rock, you have departed from iniquity, since you denied yourself and crucified the flesh with its lusts that causes you to commit iniquity.
- You have a right to name the name of Christ, AND THE LORD KNOWS YOU!

The wonderful experience for the obedient is that they received the first revelation and they know Who Jesus is. But they also received the second revelation, and Jesus knows who they are!

10

THE KINGDOM IS THE SHEEPFOLD

We compared the words of Jesus in Matthew 16 and Matthew 7 showing that knowing the identity of Jesus is intended to have us hear Christ's words and do *them*. His words regard carrying our crosses. Our humanity does not so much mind the revelation of His identity as much as our need to carry our crosses.

Let us now compare the words of Matthew 7 with John 10.

In Matthew 7, Jesus stipulated the importance of accomplishing the will of the Father in order to enter the Kingdom. Focus on the point of entering the Kingdom.

> *Matthew 7:21   Not every one that saith unto me, Lord, Lord, shall enter into the kingdom of heaven; but he that doeth the will of my Father which is in heaven.*

Then He said many will appeal to how many miracles, prophecies and deliverances from spirits they accomplished in His name. Just stop and think about this. *Many* will say this to Him.

> *Matthew 7:23-25   And then will I profess unto them, I never knew you: depart from me, ye that work iniquity. Therefore whosoever heareth these sayings of mine, and doeth*

THE KINGDOM IS THE SHEEPFOLD

> *them, I will liken him unto a wise man, which built his house upon a rock: And the rain descended, and the floods came, and the winds blew, and beat upon that house; and it fell not: for it was founded upon a rock.*

With thought of entrance into the Kingdom as our focus, consider the words of John 10.

> *John 10:1 Verily, verily, I say unto you, He that entereth not by the door into the sheepfold, but climbeth up some other way, the same is a thief and a robber.*

The theme again is entrance. Jesus likened entrance into the Kingdom with entrance into the sheepfold. The Kingdom is the sheepfold. Notice that they're people trying to get into the sheepfold who go another way. They are called thieves and robbers. The thief and robber is not the devil, but a false believer. This is important to keep in mind as we continue in John 10 because partway through this chapter a passage appears which people mistake to refer to the devil. We have just seen how the context is speaking about false believers wanting to enter the sheepfold.

> *John 10:2-4 But he that entereth in by the door is the shepherd of the sheep. To him the porter openeth; and the sheep hear his voice: and he calleth his own sheep by name, and leadeth them out. And when he putteth forth his own sheep, he goeth before them, and the sheep follow him: for they know his voice.*

Didn't Jesus say those who hear His words and obey them are those who build their houses on the rock, or in other words, are those who enter the Kingdom? Here we read the sheep know His voice.

> *John 10:5-6 And a stranger will they not follow, but will flee from him: for they know not the voice of strangers. This parable spake Jesus unto them: but they understood not what things they were which he spake unto them.*

Jesus knew they were not following His words, so he clarified what He meant.

> *John 10:7-8 Then said Jesus unto them again, Verily, verily, I say unto you, I am the door of the sheep. All that ever came before me are thieves and robbers: but the sheep did not hear them.*

This is evidence that the thief and robber is not the devil in this context. *All* who came before Jesus were thieves and robbers. Satan is an individual. In no way can this be limited to satan.

> *John 10:9-11 I am the door: by me if any man enter in, he shall be saved, and shall go in and out, and find pasture. The thief cometh not, but for to steal, and to kill, and to destroy: I am come that they might have life, and that they might have it more abundantly. I am the good shepherd: the good shepherd giveth his life for the sheep.*

Let us pay close attention to that last phrase. He gives His life for the sheep.

JESUS KNOWS HIS SHEEP

> *John 10:12-14 But he that is an hireling, and not the shepherd, whose own the sheep are not, seeth the wolf coming, and leaveth the sheep, and fleeth: and the wolf catcheth them, and scattereth the sheep. The hireling fleeth, because he is an hireling, and careth not for the sheep. I am the good shepherd,* **and know my sheep**, *and am known of mine.*

THE KINGDOM IS THE SHEEPFOLD

Didn't Jesus tell the disciples that *He never knew* the people who merely called Him Lord and performed wonders in His name? Here He says *He knows His sheep.* Only the sheep are getting in.

ONLY SHEEP ENTER THE KINGDOM

Jesus only knows those who take their crosses. He knows His sheep and *they hear Him.* He knows His sheep and they know Him.

After having said He knows His sheep and they know Him, we then read the same relationship existed with He and the Father.

> *John 10:15-16 As the Father knoweth me, even so know I the Father: and I lay down my life for the sheep. And other sheep I have, which are not of this fold: them also I must bring, and they shall hear my voice; and there shall be one fold, and one shepherd.*

Jesus then proceeded to refer to the church who would consist of both Jew and Gentile together in one body or sheepfold.

> *John 10:17-18 Therefore doth my Father love me, because I lay down my life, that I might take it again. No man taketh it from me, but I lay it down of myself. I have power to lay it down, and I have power to take it again. This commandment have I received of my Father.*

Remember that Jesus said not everyone who cries, Lord, Lord," shall enter the Kingdom, but he who does the will of His Father. Here He says the commandment from His Father is to lay His life down and take it up again. So, if His sheep follow Him, and He would lay His life down and take it up again, He is talking about carrying our crosses. A false prophet will not preach this message, or may even preach it, but will not take up his cross, himself.

A sheep is humble. The meek shall inherit the earth. Self-exaltant-spirited, and dictatorial ministers are false prophets.

THE CALL FOR THE SHEEP IS GOING FORTH

Sheep from miles around will hear this message when it is preached and will gather towards it. They hear His voice and want to continue to hear it. They recognize this message.

Wolves are not allowed into the sheepfold. They will not be there. Sheep have been butchered by wolves in false prophetic circles because they do not belong in wolves' dens. They belong in the sheepfold. And when they enter the sheepfold upon hearing this message that coincides with their spirits, they will be in safe territory where the wolves cannot harm them.

It was of the sheep's own decision that he/she walked into a den of wolves, mistakenly thinking that was the way to go. But when they finally hear the true message of Christ, something will ring true in their hearts when, they then realize, nothing else really did. When they hear Christ's voice they will then cease hearing the false prophets and follow His Word.

Hearing of the people whom Jesus knows ought to grip our hearts so strongly. I want to ensure I am one of the sheep whom He knows. I want to enter into the Kingdom. I don't want to just say, "Lord, Lord."

Recall that the revelation from the Father is possessing the knowledge that Jesus is the Son of God – it's knowing that He's Lord. And it's easy to get that revelation because Jesus said, "Many will say to me, 'Lord, Lord'." We know that having that first revelation causes us to be blessed. Jesus told Peter he was blessed because flesh and blood did not reveal that to him. Along with that revelation, we can operate in the gifts of the Spirit and the supernatural and still not enter the Kingdom and not enter the sheepfold.

THE KINGDOM IS THE SHEEPFOLD

The additional revelation that Jesus referred to, as He continued to speak to Peter, concerned informing Peter of Peter's identity, how Peter would be given keys to the Kingdom, and how the church would be built on the rock. Then He started to talk to them about the cross. From that point in time forth, when He recognized they received divine insight about His identity, they were ready for the additional revelation. He began telling them how He must suffer, be killed and rise again the third day.

Peter rebuked him and said such a thought should be as far from Jesus' mind as could be. Jesus called Peter by the name, "satan," and how much an offence such a thought is to the Lord. He then informed the rest of the disciples that if any of them does not take up their crosses, deny themselves and follow Him, they cannot be his.

Jesus knows those who are His.

THE WILL OF THE FATHER

We have to lay our lives down and lose them, so we can receive them back again. Isn't it interesting that when Jesus spoke about His sheep, the Shepherd's voice and entering the sheepfold, that He said He had power to lay his life down and to take it up again? He said the Father loved Him because He lays His life down for the sheep. He received that commandment from His Father.

He is giving forth a strong hint for us to hear His words about going to the cross so that we might realize what our mandate is.

When we talk about Christ's death, know that we died with Him by faith. His words about His burial include the truth that we were buried with Him. Take a scanned picture of Jesus on the cross, and Photoshop your face where His face was on the cross, because you died with Him. You were also resurrected with Him. That is not all. You are even ascended and seated with Him on the right hand throne in glory!

No wonder He told them to follow Him after speaking about His need to lay his life down and take it up again. We must take up our crosses, deny ourselves and thereby follow Him. That was the commandment He received of the Father, so what do you think our commandment is going to be in order for us to enter the Kingdom?

It's easy for a man to stand behind a pulpit, point his finger and demand all these self-denying experiences in our life and not do one bit of it himself. It is actually the spirit of antichrist to refuse to carry the cross. The message of Christ is the death, burial and resurrection of the cross. Paul said he preached nothing but Christ and Him crucified. Paul practiced it himself.

Paul was beaten five times with rods. One beating was intended to stop him from preaching any more, but five beatings did not stop him! He was left for dead in one instance. Some feel that when he referred to a man whom he knew fourteen years earlier, whom he did not know was in the body or out of the body, he referred to himself in the instance in which he was left dead. Thinking he was clinically dead, the persecutors left him, and it may be then that he left his body and temporarily existed in glory.

He was in shipwreck, floating on a board in the sea, showing that he indeed practiced what he preached. He did not preach the cross and demand everyone deny themselves while he walked in a rose garden. He denied himself more than any of his hearers did.

Paul taught people to not be many masters, or teachers. In other words, do not envy to be a teacher of the people, because teachers are going to be judged more carefully than the average person. And as a minister of the Word of God, I have accepted the responsibility of humbling myself and practicing what I preach more than I expect my listeners to do so.

THE KINGDOM IS THE SHEEPFOLD

THE SPIRIT OF ANTICHRIST

The spirit of antichrist is against this message of the cross. It's against self-humility. It's against self denial. This computer-chip idea of a mark on the hands and foreheads is a ruse. The real spirit of antichrist is an anti-cross message. It might be a message that is rife with the miraculous and prophetic. But the ones who are going into this Kingdom are the ones who are doing the will of His Father. They're hearing the words of Jesus and are doing something about it. We have to do something with the revelation of Jesus.

Recall that Jesus was referring to false prophets before He spoke about those who cry, "Lord, Lord" and yet do not enter the Kingdom.

> *Matthew 7:13 Enter ye in at the strait gate: for wide is the gate, and broad is the way, that leadeth to destruction, and many there be which go in thereat:*

Who did he say enter the way of destruction? Many. Is not that what he said about the amount of people who will refer Jesus to their miracles, prophecies and deliverances in His name in order to enter the Kingdom? The "many" who take the broad road to destruction are the same "many" who rely upon the miraculous to enter the Kingdom.

> *Matthew 7:14 Because strait is the gate, and narrow is the way, which leadeth unto life, and few there be that find it.*

Few enter the sheepfold and Kingdom compared with the many who do not. And this is speaking of people who profess Christianity! It is not talking about the world population as a whole. The many who cry "Lord" are the many amongst the church world who take the broad way to destruction.

SHEEP AND WOLVES

Matthew 7:15 Beware of false prophets, which come to you in sheep's clothing, but inwardly they are ravening wolves.

What was John 10 talking about? Sheep. The sheep whom He knows are those who take the narrow path to Life. The false prophets are those who perform wonders and yet do not carry their crosses. They received the first revelation of Christ's identity, but effectively rejected the second from the Son as Peter initially did.

The term "sheep" comes up in Matthew 7 just as it did in John 10. It is because there are wolves dressed in sheep's clothing that causes them to call Jesus Lord. A sheep calls Jesus "Lord". To be dressed in sheep's clothing, therefore, requires them to call Jesus Lord. Sheep cast out devils, perform wonders and prophesy in the name of Jesus. Jesus is not saying that all the people who perform wonders and cast out devils are false prophets. No, He told his disciples to do those things. True sheep accomplish those things, but the wolves deceive people by doing the same things in the name of Jesus. But there is one thing the wolves won't do – the will of the Father. They will not hear Jesus' words about the cross and do them.

Now, these wolves may not necessarily feel they are false. These people genuinely thought they could enter the Kingdom based upon their miraculous deeds. But they are deceived. False prophets often do not know they are false.

2 Timothy 3:13 But evil men and seducers shall wax worse and worse, deceiving, **and being deceived.**

If we knew who these false people were, and asked them if they believe Jesus is Lord they would reply most affirmatively. However, if you told them that did not mean they were in the Kingdom, they would be appalled at such a thought. They might even appeal to the same thing that those whom Jesus rejected

THE KINGDOM IS THE SHEEPFOLD

appealed to – the miraculous. You might proceed to tell them there is the additional revelation from the Son of God that one requires for Kingdom access – self-denial, taking up the cross and following Jesus. Such people would reject this notion.

Listen for the message of the cross. If it is a crossless message, then false prophecy is going on. You will not know who the false prophets are by their gifts, but by their fruit. The fruit of the Spirit grows the more you deny your flesh what it wants, because the fleshliness in our lives hinders the Spirit from growing forth in fruit. The spirit of antichrist will have nothing to do with self denial.

Jesus contrasted sheep from wolves before He spoke of the many who are disallowed entrance into the Kingdom. Few there be that follow the narrow path to Life. This informs us that the Kingdom is Life and is the Sheepfold.

You can actually reason why people might think they are in good terms with Jesus if they are successfully performing wonders in His name. But that is not the way it is. The cross must be involved in our lives. He wants to know us in order to allow us into His kingdom, not see the performance of many supernaturally gifts. He never knew these miracle workers but He said He knows His sheep.

Notice that Jesus was called a lamb who was led dumb to the slaughter. The sheep is a most defenceless creature. When a sheep knows you are taking it to its death, it will not bite nor kick to defend itself. Jesus compared Himself with a sheep because He denied Himself and did not defend Himself. He knew He had to die and He accepted that. Self is no longer an issue when someone has accepted the cross.

In order to determine if we are one of the few who carry their crosses and enter the sheepfold of the Kingdom we must analyze how much we defend ourselves when self is attacked by others. When one truly builds his/her house on the rock, the reason the house is not destroyed by the storms of life is because the part of us that can be destroyed has already been denied – self.

Jesus was ready to be crucified and exclaimed...

> John 14:30 *Hereafter I will not talk much with you: for the prince of this world cometh, and hath nothing in me.*

He said the devil had nothing in Him because the means in people's lives by which the devil has opportunity against Him was denied by Jesus – self-exaltation and self-life. Our flesh was made from the dust of the earth. The serpent was cursed in Eden to eat the dust of the earth. In other words, he feeds upon our fleshliness and that which Jesus said must be denied in order to follow Him. The Lord did not tell us these things so that He might enjoy watching us grovel, but rather to remove the food in our lives upon which the devil thrives. The devil had nothing in the flesh of Jesus Christ by which he could take opportunity to tear Him down and ruin His God-called purpose.

This is also the reason why the hireling flees when he sees the wolf coming. He does not deny himself. He does not carry his cross. The shepherd lays his life down for the sheep. Jesus had such confidence that laying down His life would enable Him to later take it up again When He would take it up again, it would be an immortal Life that could not be killed again.

THE CROSS REMOVES THAT WHICH THE DEVIL TAKES ADVANTAGE OF

To truly take up our crosses, we require a confidence that everything is going to be alright in the long run. Laying down our lives is going to be rewarded with taking them up again unto eternal life. Jesus had that confidence. If we lose our lives, He said, we will find them again.

You might not feel that confident yet and you may be struggling in this area. The Lord knows it is a journey and it requires time for us to learn these things. So do not fret. Just be willing to learn.

THE KINGDOM IS THE SHEEPFOLD

John 10:14   I am the good shepherd, and know my sheep, and am known of mine.

Many know Him, but the important part is whether or not He knows them. He does not know those whom He said are workers of iniquity. His further words about a wise man hearing his words and doing them, therefore, are words that have something to do with causing us to not be workers of iniquity. They have to do with ensuring we are not wolves.

ARE WE SURE WE ARE NOT WOLVES?

One way in which to discern whether or not we are wolves is to consider whether or not we tear up other sheep.

Paul told the Galatians that if they manifested works of the flesh, they would not inherit the Kingdom. This is what we are discussing! In that same chapter he said that we had better be careful that when we bite and fuss with each other, we do not devour one another. The context was works of the flesh as opposed to fruit of the Spirit (Gal. 5:14-23). Then he said those who are Christ's – the sheep whom He knows – have crucified the flesh with its lusts thereof (Gal. 5:24).

Half of the scars that believers bear were never taken from the devil's works against us, but from wolves in the church whom we trusted as sheep. When we get hurt, let us watch out lest we retaliate. When we retaliate we lower ourselves to their level and become wolves, too.

John 10:27-28   My sheep hear my voice, and I know them, and they follow me: And I give unto them eternal life; and they shall never perish, neither shall any man pluck them out of my hand.

Matthew 16:25   For whosoever will save his life shall lose it: and whosoever will lose his life for my sake shall find it.

> *John 10:10 The thief cometh not, but for to steal, and to kill, and to destroy: I am come that they might have life, and that they might have it more abundantly.*

The more abundant life is the greater form of resurrection life that can never die again. This is what we receive when we are willing to carry our crosses and deny ourselves. This kind of death and loss of life leads to a resurrection form of life that cannot die again. When we follow Him and die in the same self denial He experienced, the resurrection life He gives to us is far more abundant life than our natural lives ever possessed.

Jesus rebuked hypocritical religious leaders who put heavy burdens on their followers and would take none of it themselves (Matt. 23:4).

The devil can only appeal to the flesh that Jesus instructs us to deny and crucify. Jesus wants us to become invincible by denying the thing the devil feeds upon. We must deny self until the devil has nothing in us with which he can appeal and hold sway over us.

In the book of Revelation John was told to see a Lion of Judah and actually saw a lamb standing as it had been slain. Why did the voice say that the Lamb was a Lion? It was because Jesus' act of the greatest self denial in giving His life in death accomplished the boldest conclusion of victory.

> *John 10:4 And when he putteth forth his own sheep, he goeth before them, and the sheep follow him: for they know his voice.*

"Peter, I have an additional revelation for you. You know who I am. The Father revealed this to you. But I've got something else for you to hear. What I have to say to you will put you on a rock so that not even the gates of hell can withstand you. Take up your cross and follow me."

11

THE KINGDOM MOUNTAIN OF ZION

There is a wonderful visionary representation of the entire concept of knowing Christ and building our houses on the Rock. It is found in the Book of Revelation. (The Book of Revelation is far more than just information about the end of the world!)

> *Revelation 14:1-8 And I looked, and, lo,* **a Lamb stood on the mount Sion, and with him an hundred forty and four thousand,** *having* **his Father's name written in their foreheads.** *And I heard a voice from heaven, as the voice of many waters, and as the voice of a great thunder: and I heard the voice of harpers harping with their harps: And they sung as it were a new song before the throne, and before the four beasts, and the elders: and no man could learn that song but the hundred and forty and four thousand, which were redeemed from the earth. These are they which were not defiled with women; for they are virgins. These are they which follow the Lamb whithersoever he goeth. These were redeemed from among men, being the firstfruits unto God and to the Lamb. And in their mouth was found no guile: for they are without fault before the throne of God. And I saw another angel fly in the midst of heaven, having the everlasting gospel to preach unto them that dwell on the earth, and to every nation, and kindred, and tongue, and people,*

> *Saying with a loud voice, Fear God, and give glory to him; for the hour of his judgment is come: and worship him that made heaven, and earth, and the sea, and the fountains of waters. (8) And there followed another angel, saying,* **Babylon is fallen, is fallen***, that great city, because she made all nations drink of the wine of the wrath of her fornication.*

Jesus said the disciples had to *follow Him* in order to be part of the church on the Rock. This would prohibit the *gates of death* from holding them back. They receive *resurrection power* from their union to Jesus, the Rock.

In Revelation 14, Jesus is seen as a Lamb in John's vision for this very reason. He was *sacrificed* as a Lamb when he died on the cross for our sins. He took up His cross and died, only to resurrect. That Lamb **stood** on *a* **rock** called Mount Zion. Believers **stood** with Him!

Do not miss the point in John's vision. Notice the Lamb's Father's name is written on their foreheads. The forehead was used in scripture to refer to a person's **will**.

> *Ezekiel 3:8-9   Behold, I have made thy face strong against their faces, and thy* **forehead** *strong against their* **foreheads***. As an adamant harder than flint have I made thy* **forehead***: fear them not, neither be dismayed at their looks, though they be a rebellious house.*

God would make Ezekiel's **will** more unmoving to preach the truth than the will of the rebels who were unmoved to obey God. With that in mind, what better way to symbolize willingness to do *the will of the Father* than to have *the Father's name on one's forehead?*

Jesus said the only people who will enter the Kingdom are the people who do the will of the Father. Those who do the Father's will – which is what Jesus called obedience to His own Words – are like those who build their houses on rock. Their houses stand when the storms and waves crash upon them.

THE KINGDOM MOUNTAIN OF ZION

Likewise, these 144,000 *stand* with Jesus on *the Rock of Mount Zion.*

Not only that, but there are those who do not do the Father's will and build on sand, causing their houses to fall.

> *Revelation 14:8 And there followed another angel, saying,* **Babylon is fallen, is fallen***, that great city, because she made all nations drink of the wine of the wrath of her fornication.*

Notice the traits borne by the 144,000:

> *Revelation 14:4 These are they which were not defiled with women; for* **they are virgins***. These are they which* **follow the Lamb** *whithersoever he goeth. These were redeemed from among men, being the* **firstfruits** *unto God and to the Lamb.*

VIRGINS

> *2 Corinthians 11:2 For I am jealous over you with godly jealousy: for I have espoused you to one husband, that I* **may present you as a chaste virgin to Christ***.*

FOLLOW HIM

> *Matthew 16:24 Then said Jesus unto his disciples, If any man will come after me, let him deny himself, and take up his cross, and* **follow me***.*

FIRSTFRUITS

> *James 1:18 Of his own will begat he us with the word of truth, that* **we should be a kind of firstfruits of his creatures***.*

A Pattern of Hearing One Thing, But Seeing Another

Revelation 7 also speaks of this group of 144,000, explaining that they are 12,000 from each of the 12 tribes of Israel. However, notice a pattern here in this very highly symbolic Book of Revelation. John first *heard* the number.

> *Revelation 7:4* **And I heard the number** *of them which were sealed: and there were sealed an hundred and forty and four thousand of all the tribes of the children of Israel.*

After He **heard** this number, look what he **saw**:

> *Revelation 7:9-10 After this* **I beheld, and, lo**, *a great multitude, which no man could number, of all nations, and kindreds, and people, and tongues, stood before the throne, and before the Lamb, clothed with white robes, and palms in their hands; And cried with a loud voice, saying, Salvation to our God which sitteth upon the throne, and unto the Lamb.*

When we read back a little further in the Book of Revelation, we find that John *heard* something else, but the same thing he then *saw* turned out to be quite different from the description he *heard*:

> *Revelation 5:5-6 And one of the elders* **saith unto me**, *Weep not:* **behold, the Lion of the tribe of Juda**, *the Root of David, hath prevailed to open the book, and to loose the seven seals thereof. And* **I beheld, and, lo**, *in the midst of the throne and of the four beasts, and in the midst of the elders, stood* **a Lamb as it had been slain**, *having seven horns and seven eyes, which are the seven Spirits of God sent forth into all the earth.*

He *heard* words about a lion, but when he turned to *see* this Lion, he *saw* a lamb standing as though it was slain and resurrected from the dead! This is the same pattern we read in chapter 7. The reason the Lamb was called a Lion was due to the most courageous and lion-like act that Jesus ever did which was to be obedient in His lamb-like death of the cross. Sacrificing Himself like a silent lamb to the slaughter was done with the boldness of a lion! Not only that, but Christ was of the tribe of Judah whose emblem was the grand lion.

What John *heard* was the *spiritual reality* of what *looked* like the most opposite picture of that reality.

John *heard* about 12,000 from each tribe of Israel, making 144,000. But when he actually *saw* the people just described, they were the *Church* from *every nation*, and were without number. The number 144,000 is the result of multiplying 12 by 12 by 1000. The church is the called *the Israel of God*.

> *Galatians 6:16   And as many as walk according to this rule, peace be on them, and mercy, and upon the Israel of God.*

THE CHURCH IS ISRAEL WITH GENTILES ADDED

The Church is the New Israel! Israel and Judah were prophesied to receive a new covenant wherein the law of God would be put within their hearts (Jeremiah 31:31-34). This is precisely the New Covenant we now enjoy, as Paul described the law written within our hearts (2 Corinthians 3:3; Hebrews 8:10; 10:16). It's just that the Gentiles were allowed into this covenant with Israel for the first time without having to convert and become Jews.

The Church did not *replace* Israel, but *is* Israel in the New Covenant joined by all believing Gentiles. Many mistaken this notion and call it "Replacement Theology," but that is not the case at all. Nothing *replaced* anything. The New Covenant was promised to Israel and Judah following the Old Covenant. For the first time in history God opened Israel's next covenant up to the entire Gentile world. We Gentiles actually *joined* Israel as far as God is concerned, and the New Covenant is for both Jew and Gentile to be reconciled *together* in one body by the cross of Jesus Christ (Ephesians 2:11-22).

Revelation 14 relates a vision of people using a spiritual number of 144,000 who *followed* the Lamb, indicating they *followed Him with a cross*. Jesus told us to take up our crosses and follow Him. Otherwise we cannot be His disciples. *These people stand* on a Rock just as Jesus said the Church is built on a Rock.

THE ROCK OF ZION – GOD'S KINGDOM

Jesus rules in His Kingdom from this Mount Zion in Revelation 14.

> *Psalms 110:1-2 A Psalm of David. The LORD said unto my Lord, Sit thou at my right hand, until I make thine enemies thy footstool. The LORD shall send* **the rod of thy strength out of Zion:** *rule thou in the midst of thine enemies.*

The Rock, therefore, stands for Jesus, Himself, as well as His Kingdom. Did you notice that the Psalm said Jesus Christ's strength is out of Zion? That is where the Lamb *stood* with the 144,000!

> *Hebrews 12:22 But ye are come unto mount Sion, and unto the city of the living God, the heavenly Jerusalem, and to an innumerable company of angels,*

During his rule, David reigned from the location of Mount Zion which he captured from the Jebusites. Zion was a mountain inside the city Jerusalem at the southwest part of the city. When David captured it, he called it the City of David, and it stood like a city within a city (2 Samuel 5:6-9)!

THE KINGDOM MOUNTAIN OF ZION

Some feel Jesus is not on the throne of David yet because David had a physical throne located on the Earth, and Jesus is not seated anywhere on a throne in the Earth today. But Psalm 110 connects the place where Jesus is presently at the right hand of the Father with being on Mount Zion! David's earthly Zion was a shadow of the true Mount Zion in Heaven where Jesus' throne is presently situated! Those who think Jesus is not yet ruling on the throne of David have considered the wrong connection. It's not the fact that David sat on the throne in the Earth that we are intended to consider when thinking of the throne of David, but that David's throne was on Mt. Zion. Jesus is on the spiritual Mt. Zion right now, according to Psalm 110. That means He rules from the throne of David. Peter said that Psalm 110 was fulfilled when Jesus ascended into glory and sat down at the right hand throne (Acts 2:29-35). There was an earthly Zion and there is a spiritual Zion. There is likewise an earthly Jerusalem and a heavenly Jerusalem. Jesus is indeed on the throne of David now!

> *Acts 2:29-33 Men and brethren, let me freely speak unto you of the patriarch David, that he is both dead and buried, and his sepulchre is with us unto this day. Therefore being a prophet, and knowing that God had sworn with an oath to him, that of the fruit of his loins, according to the flesh, he would raise up Christ to sit on his throne; He seeing this before spake of the resurrection of Christ, that his soul was not left in hell, neither his flesh did see corruption. This Jesus hath God raised up, whereof we all are witnesses. Therefore being by the right hand of God exalted, and having received of the Father the promise of the Holy Ghost, he hath shed forth this, which ye now see and hear.*

Revelation 14 is God's means of relating to us the truth that we are in the Kingdom and rule and reign with Jesus on Mount Zion. The Church is on this Rock called Zion. The 144,000 stand on Zion with the Lamb who was slain and yet came forth standing! This power over death and the grave is resurrection power, and the Lord's strength is sent forth from the Rock Zion according to Psalm 110:2.

These saints are with the Lamb, and have followed that Lamb wherever He went. Notice the focus upon *following Him wherever He went*. When He spoke to the disciples in Matthew 16 about building His Church on the Rock of Himself, or His Kingdom which is on Zion, He said they must take up their crosses and follow Him. All of this is what Revelation 14's vision is trying to relate to us!

THE DEGREE OF POWER TOWARD US IS RESURRECTION POWER

In the following passage, Paul explained that the right hand seating of Psalm 110 was fulfilled by Jesus Christ after His resurrection, and said that there was **a power towards us that matches the degree of resurrection power used to put Christ on that throne.** Do not miss this! The degree of the power of God towards us – at our disposal – is equal to the degree of power wherewith God raised up Christ and set Him on the right hand throne of power. It's *according to*. It's the same degree of power.

> *Ephesians 1:18-23 The eyes of your understanding being enlightened; that ye may know what is the hope of his calling, and what the riches of the glory of his inheritance in the saints, And* **what is the exceeding greatness of his power to us-ward who believe, according to the working of his mighty power, Which he wrought in Christ, when he raised him from the dead, and set him at his own right hand in the heavenly places,** *Far above all principality, and power, and might, and dominion, and every name that is named, not only in this world, but also in that which is to come: And hath put all things under his feet, and gave him to be the head*

over all things to the church, Which is his body, the fulness of him that filleth all in all.

Notice the Church is called the body of Jesus Christ, just as the 5th chapter of Ephesians explained Eve was bone of Adam's bone and flesh of His flesh (Eph. 5:30-32). The resurrection power that placed Christ on this throne is ***"towards us"***. The idea of *union* to the Church is involved in all of this.

> *Ephesians 2:5-6 Even when we were dead in sins, hath quickened us together with Christ, (by grace ye are saved;) And* **hath raised us up together, and made us sit together in heavenly places in Christ Jesus:**

The reason that the gates of the *grave* cannot prevail against the Church is because *resurrection* power is given to us as the result of Christ being seated on the right hand throne. Since the power working towards us is equal to the power by which God *resurrected* Jesus and set Him on the throne, it is *resurrection* power that is towards us. He sends forth His power of *resurrection life* out of Zion from the right hand throne. For this reason, the gates of the *grave* cannot prevail against the church that is on the Rock!

Notice the flow of thought between the following passages:

> *2 Timothy 2:19 Nevertheless the* **foundation** *[Upon this Rock I will build my Church] of God standeth sure [The house on rock stood, the house on sand fell], having this seal,* **The Lord knoweth them** *that are his ["Depart from me, I never knew you"]. And, Let every one that nameth* **the name of Christ depart from iniquity.**

> *Matthew 16:16-17 And Simon Peter answered and said,* **Thou art the Christ, the Son of the living God** *[Let every one that nameth the name of Christ]. And Jesus answered and said unto him, Blessed art thou, Simon Barjona:* **for flesh and blood hath not**

> revealed it unto thee, but my Father which is in heaven.
>
> Matthew 7:2-23 Not every one that saith unto me, Lord, Lord, *[1 Tim. 2:19 Let every one that nameth the name of Christ...]* shall enter into the kingdom of heaven; but he that doeth the will of my Father which is in heaven. Many will say to me in that day, Lord, Lord, have we not prophesied in thy name? and in thy name have cast out devils? and in thy name done many wonderful works? And then will I profess unto them, I never knew you: depart from me, ye that work iniquity. *[1 Tim. 2:19 Let every one that nameth the name of Christ depart from iniquity]*
>
> Matthew 16:18 And I say also unto thee, ...
>
> Matthew 7:24 Therefore **whosoever heareth these sayings of mine, and doeth them**, I will liken him unto a wise man, which built his house upon a rock:

If we do not hear the words of Jesus, and truly honour Him as Lord by obeying His words, we will not depart from iniquity, but we will depart *from Him*.

In Paul's letter to Timothy we read about the *foundation* and the same details Jesus emphasized to the disciples in Matthew 7 concerning Jesus *knowing* people and the issue of working *iniquity*. Earlier in 2 Timothy 2, we read...

> 2 Timothy 2:8-13 Remember that **Jesus Christ of the seed of David was raised from the dead** according to my gospel: Wherein I suffer trouble, as an evil doer, even unto bonds; but the word of God is not bound. Therefore I endure all things for the elect's sakes, that they may also obtain the salvation which is in Christ Jesus with eternal glory. It is a faithful saying: **For if we be dead with him, we shall also live with him: If we suffer, we**

THE KINGDOM MOUNTAIN OF ZION

shall also reign with him: if we deny him, he also will deny us: If we believe not, yet he abideth faithful: he cannot deny himself.

If we suffer with Him, we shall reign with Him. He rules as son of David on David's throne, resurrected and sitting at the right hand of power. These 144,000 *followed* Him through the death of the cross and self denial, and therefore *suffered* so that they can resurrect and *reign* with Him and *stand* on Mount Zion – the Kingdom Mountain of Jesus Christ!

Revelation 1:5-6 And from Jesus Christ, who is the faithful witness, and **the first begotten of the dead,** *and the prince of the kings of the earth. Unto him that loved us, and washed us from our sins in his own blood, And* **hath made us kings and priests** *unto God and his Father; to him be glory and dominion for ever and ever. Amen.*

His resurrection status as first begotten *of the dead,* precedes the truth that we are **kings and priests with Jesus Christ**. We stand with Him, the resurrected Lamb, on the Rock of the Kingdom mountain of Zion. While we *stand*, we read of others *falling* – not *standing* – in destruction due to disregarding the instruction from Jesus to take up their crosses and follow Him.

Revelation 14:8 And there followed another angel, saying, Babylon is **fallen, is fallen***, that great city, because she made all nations drink of the wine of the wrath of her fornication.*

Did not Jesus say those who refuse to hear His words and do them are like fools who build houses on sand whose houses *fall?* Babylon was literally built in the desert *sands* of Mesopotamia in Iraq. As Babylon *falls*, those on the Rock of Zion remain *standing* firm!

The Church obeys the Father's will, so they are represented as having their Father's name on their foreheads. Instead of the *mark of the beast* on their foreheads, the 144,000 have the Father's name on their foreheads.

12

MOUNT ZION'S TRANSFIGURING GLORY

> *Matthew 17:1-5 And after six days Jesus taketh Peter, James, and John his brother, and bringeth them up into an high mountain apart, And was transfigured before them: and his face did shine as the sun, and his raiment was white as the light. And, behold, there appeared unto them Moses and Elias talking with him. Then answered Peter, and said unto Jesus, Lord, it is good for us to be here: if thou wilt, let us make here three Tabernacles; one for thee, and one for Moses, and one for Elias. While he yet spake, behold, a bright cloud overshadowed them: and behold a voice out of the cloud, which said, This is my beloved Son, in whom I am well pleased; hear ye him.*

Following Matthew 16's account of the revelation of the Father and the revelation of the Son, the very next chapter lays this concept out all over again. But it does it by way of an object lesson. Jesus took the disciples into a *high mountain*. Sounds like a rock! On this mountain, Jesus was *transfigured*.

Moses and Elijah appeared there with Jesus notice what they talked about.

> *Luke 9:30-31 And, behold, there talked with him two men, which were Moses and Elias: (31) Who appeared in*

glory, and spake of his decease which he should accomplish at Jerusalem.

They spoke with Him about the cross!

THE IMPORTANCE OF HEARING ABOUT THE CROSS

What was it that Jesus began to speak to the disciples about after Peter got a revelation from the Father about His identity, in Matthew 16?

> *Matthew 16:21   From that time forth began Jesus to shew unto his disciples, how that he must go unto Jerusalem, and suffer many things of the elders and chief priests and scribes, and be killed, and be raised again the third day.*

It was the cross! What did Peter do when he heard Jesus speak about the cross?

> *Matthew 16:22   Then Peter took him, and began to rebuke him, saying, Be it far from thee, Lord: this shall not be unto thee.*

If you read carefully, the same reaction Peter had initially regarding the thoughts of Christ's cross was still in his heart. Look what happened after Peter heard Jesus speaking of the cross to Moses and Elijah:

> *Matthew 17:4   Then answered Peter, and said unto Jesus, Lord, it is good for us to be here: if thou wilt, let us make here three Tabernacles; one for thee, and one for Moses, and one for Elias.*

MOUNT ZION'S TRANSFIGURING GLORY

Peter effectively told Him to forget about going to Jerusalem. He still rejected the notion of the cross. Despite Jesus' rebuke a week earlier, Peter still did not get this second revelation. Not only that, but speaking of building a Church on the Rock, Peter suggested they *build Tabernacles on that mountain.* It was as though Peter said, "Well, Lord, you mentioned You would build the church on the rock. We're on a big rock right now, and here are Moses and Elijah. Why not build three Tabernacles on this mountain and *stay here?"*

Staying there would not only be avoiding the journey to Jerusalem where Jesus revealed He would die, but Jesus had not intended them to think about a physical house on a physical rock. He spoke about building His people, the Church of "called out people," on the Rock of His Kingdom. That would require the death and resurrection that Peter tried to avoid.

And look what happened after this. Recall that the sequence of revelations was (1) the Father gave a revelation of Christ's identity and (2) then Jesus revealed the plan of the cross and resurrection from the dead. That same sequence of revelations commences all over again on top of the mount of Transfiguration.

Matthew 17:5 While he yet spake, behold, a bright cloud overshadowed them: and behold a voice out of the cloud, which said, **This is my beloved Son***, in whom I am well pleased;* **hear ye him.**

The Father once again provided the same revelation, and revealed Christ's identity. Then He told Peter to hear what the Son had to then say. It's as though the entire sequence of revelations had to be given all over again to Peter, since Peter refused the revelation of the Son even after being rebuked a week earlier about it. While the Father told Peter to hear what the Son was saying, notice what the Son was talking about with Moses and Elijah. His death. The cross. In other words, the Father urged Peter to hear this revelation of the cross all over again, and get it this time. In fact, Jesus even speaks explicitly of the cross some more.

> Matthew 17:9 *And as they came down from the mountain, Jesus charged them, saying, Tell the vision to no man, until* **the Son of man be risen again from the dead.**

> Matthew 17:12 *But I say unto you, That Elias is come already, and they knew him not, but have done unto him whatsoever they listed.* **Likewise shall also the Son of man suffer of them.**

OUR NEED TO DENY SELF

The Kingdom Mountain cannot be our foundation and experience unless we suffer with Him.

> 2 Timothy 2:11-12 *It is a faithful saying: For if we be dead with him, we shall also live with him: (12) If we suffer, we shall also reign with him: if we deny him,* **he also will deny us:** *["I never knew you, depart from me ye workers of iniquity"]*

We do not deny Jesus by rejecting His identity. We may accept His identity but still deny Him by rejecting our need for His cross so that we might follow Him. Refusing to follow Him is actually denying Him.

The wonderful thing about this is that the transfiguration of Jesus on this mountain, or Rock, *represents the transformation that occurs in our lives when we are built upon the rock.* The revelation of the cross and the power of resurrection actually transforms our lives into overcomers!

The real house on the rock is not a physical structure. It is one's life. The Church is not the building we congregate in each week, but is a term that is defined as "called out people." The

MOUNT ZION'S TRANSFIGURING GLORY

Church is the people who have taken up their crosses to follow Jesus.

Notice that *sacrifice* is associated with transformation, and keep in mind that sacrifice means *death*, the very thing Peter tried to avoid:

> Romans 12:1-3   I beseech you therefore, brethren, by the mercies of God, that ye present your bodies a **living sacrifice**, holy, acceptable unto God, which is your reasonable service. And be not conformed to this world: but **be ye transformed by the renewing of your mind**, that ye may prove what is that good, and acceptable, and perfect, **will of God**. For I say, through the grace given unto me, to every man that is among you, not to think of himself more highly than he ought to think; but to think soberly, according as God hath dealt to every man the measure of faith.

Not only do we read about sacrifice, but transformation is mentioned along with proving the will of God! Jesus said we must do more than call Him, "Lord." We must enter the Kingdom by doing the will of the Father. Renewing our minds is getting the concept of *sacrifice of self* into our thinking. But we are called *living sacrifices*. We live a life of sacrifice in self denial. One would think a sacrifice is something that is dead! After all, sacrificing something is killing it and offering it to the Lord. However, when we sacrifice our *self life* by denying ourselves and taking up our crosses every day of our lives, you can see how we are *living* sacrifices.

Jesus told the disciples to lose their lives for His sake. That is actually losing your old way of thinking. The Greek term translated as "life" is the same Greek word translated as "soul" – "psuche." We *transliterate* that word into English as psyche, or the mind. That is the reason Romans 12 spoke of renewing the mind.

The Vital Need for "I Say Also Unto Thee"

So we have Matthew 7's Rock, Kingdom entrance and the Son's sayings all associated with Matthew 16's Church on the Rock and Christ's words, "I say also unto thee" all found in Romans 12's words from Paul to the Church. These are all seen again in Matthew 17's account of the Mount of Transfiguration where the Father gave Jesus' identity and tells Peter to hear what the Son has to say about the cross.

Romans emphasizes just what it means to *think* about the cross concept. Be a living sacrifice.

The Greek word translated as "transformed" in Romans 12:2 is the same word translated as "transfigured" in Matthew 17:2. This is enlightening! The very experience of Jesus on the Rock or Mountain of Transfiguration is what we are intended to experience by a renewing of our minds. We can see how Peter's mind required much renewing! He refused to be transformed since he was so conformed to the world. The world lives by the rule of no self-denial. In fact, the way of the world is exalt self and "look out for number 1."

This Mountain of Transfiguration is actually Mount Zion, the Kingdom Mountain of God!

13

SHINING IN KINGDOM GLORY

Peter was caught in the middle of the entire episode of the two great Kingdom revelations for the Church. This very same man wrote the following words that directly refer to his experience with Jesus on the Mount of Transfiguration. Thanks to Peter's epistle, we know that he eventually finally got Christ's revelation and lived by it wholeheartedly.

> *2 Peter 1:2-11 Grace and peace be multiplied unto you through the knowledge of God, and of Jesus our Lord, According as his divine power hath given unto us all things that pertain unto life and godliness, through the knowledge of him that hath called us to glory and virtue: Whereby are given unto us exceeding great and precious promises: that by these ye might be partakers of the divine nature, having escaped the corruption that is in the world through lust. And beside this, giving all diligence, add to your faith virtue; and to virtue knowledge; And to knowledge temperance; and to temperance patience; and to patience godliness; And to godliness brotherly kindness; and to brotherly kindness charity. For if these things be in you, and abound, they make you that ye shall neither be barren nor unfruitful in the knowledge of our Lord Jesus Christ. But he that lacketh these things is blind, and cannot see afar off, and hath forgotten that he was purged from his old sins. Wherefore the rather, brethren, give diligence to* **make your calling and**

> *election sure: for if ye do these things, ye shall never fall: For so an entrance shall be ministered unto you abundantly into the everlasting kingdom of our Lord and Saviour Jesus Christ.*

Both Jesus and Peter spoke about our need to come into a place in which we shall never fall. Jesus said that a man who hears His words and obeys them is a wise man who builds his house on a rock. The storms of life cannot cause such a house to fall. Peter listed seven elements of holiness that will cause us to never fall. Both mentioned entrance into the Kingdom.

A House is Only as Stable as its Foundation

Peter made specific mention of the divine nature. He said, "Whereby are given unto us exceeding great and precious promises: **that by these ye might be partakers of the divine nature**, having escaped the corruption that is in the world through lust." This corresponds to the fact that a house shares the stability of the rock upon which it is built. The house takes on the stable nature of the rock. Likewise, we can partake of **the divine nature** of Jesus Christ. This does not mean we become gods. It means we truly become images of God. Like houses built on rock that cannot fall, we become images of Jesus Christ in resurrection power.

Our House is Our Calling and Election

Just as Jesus told us to hear His words and do them, Peter makes the same point. His words **establish** us. They put us on a strong foundation.

> *2 Peter 1:12-18 Wherefore I will not be negligent to put you always in remembrance of these things, though ye know them,* **and be established in the present truth.** *Yea, I think it meet, as long as I am in this Tabernacle, to stir you*

SHINING IN KINGDOM GLORY

> *up by putting you in remembrance; Knowing that shortly I must put off this my Tabernacle, even as our Lord Jesus Christ hath shewed me. Moreover I will endeavour that ye may be able after my decease to* **have these things always in remembrance.** *For we have not followed cunningly devised fables, when we made known unto you the power and coming of our Lord Jesus Christ,* **but were eyewitnesses of his majesty. For he received from God the Father honour and glory, when there came such a voice to him from the excellent glory, This is my beloved Son, in whom I am well pleased. And this voice which came from heaven we heard, when we were with him in the holy mount.**

Peter made direct reference to the words of the Father on Mount Transfiguration when God said, "This is my beloved Son, hear ye Him." Just as God told Peter to hear those words about the cross, Peter wrote for his readers to heed his words and keep them always in remembrance. Peter said this while explaining how to **make our calling and election sure.** The house that is built on the Rock is our calling and election!

When we hear Jesus' words and obey them by taking up our crosses and following Him, we are making our callings and elections sure like a house on a rock that cannot fall. Making something **sure** is making it secure and solid on a good foundation. An entrance into the Kingdom will be granted to us abundantly as a result.

> *Matthew 7:21   Not every one that saith unto me, Lord, Lord, shall* **enter into the kingdom of heaven;** *but he that doeth the will of my Father which is in heaven.*

> *2 Peter 1:11   For so an* **entrance** *shall be ministered unto you abundantly* **into the everlasting kingdom** *of our Lord and Saviour Jesus Christ.*

Peter connected the concept of Christ's words concerning entrance into the Kingdom with His words about the houses built on rock with the picture of Christ's transfiguration. He took the thought of entering the Kingdom from Matthew 7:21, and coupled it with the thought of Matthew 17's Mountain of Transfiguration.

Recall that Peter initially had the idea of building the house on the Rock all wrong. It was not to be a physical house of wood and nails, but rather the wood and nails of the work of the cross in our very lives, so to speak. We build our lives upon the **words** and teachings of Jesus Christ regarding the truths of the cross and our need to carry our own crosses.

The entire concept of the Kingdom of Mount Zion and the truths of Christ and His cross are actually synonymous.

THE KEY TO BEING KNOWN BY JESUS

If doing the Father's will causes us to enter the Kingdom, and Jesus' recognition of us likewise brings us into the Kingdom, then obviously obedience of the Father's will causes Jesus to know us. This is connected to something Peter wrote. He said we actually partake of the divine nature if we heed these truths.

> *2 Peter 1:4 Whereby are given unto us exceeding great and precious promises: that by these ye might be partakers of the divine nature, having escaped the corruption that is in the world through lust.*

This means we are changed into the image of God. We, as Jesus was, are transfigured, or transformed! It all occurs by the grand renewal of the mind.

Peter was there when the Father spoke of Jesus being His Son. While they were on the mountain of transfiguration, Peter heard God tell him to listen to Jesus' words about his decease. Notice what Peter then wrote:

SHINING IN KINGDOM GLORY

2 Peter 1:19 We have also ***a more sure word*** *of prophecy; whereunto ye do well that ye* ***take heed, as unto a light that shineth in a dark place****, until the day dawn, and the day star arise in your hearts:*

SHINING IN HIS GLORY

The ***more sure word of prophecy*** is a word that puts you on a sure foundation. In fact, that word, itself, is the sure foundation. Peter related what he finally received, himself, after having rejected it at the first. He said this ***sure word*** is like a light that shines in a dark place. It shines and shines until finally something happens. Something transforms and transfigures! The day dawns! The daystar actually arises in our hearts! It shone on us until something powerful occurred and ***we began shining!***

Jesus' face shone like the sun that day (Matt. 17:2). Peter told us to take heed to His words that are like a light that shines in a dark place. That light will shine so powerfully until it actually causes us to start shining, ourselves! The wonder of it all is that Jesus Christ was said to transfigure, or transform when He began shining like the sun. That is the same Greek word Paul used to teach us how we must be transformed by the renewing of our minds. The picture is clear! The light that shone from Jesus' face represents the truths He spoke about concerning the self-denial of the cross. Refusal to save our souls or lives is refusing to change our way of thinking. The soul is the Greek term "psuche," or our ***psyche***. Refusal to change our old way of thinking is self-preservation and refusal to take up our crosses and follow Him. It is a manner of thinking. Jesus did not mean for us to literally carry a wooden cross every day, but to change our concept and cease exalting self.

Unless we deny ourselves, we actually hinder His Spirit from working out from within our lives. Ministry is inhibited. Too much of ***us*** comes forth and not enough of Him. He is in us.

His Spirit needs free course to manifest from our lives in vibrant spiritual ministry.

When we acquire this way of thinking, it will transfigure or transform our lives as well!

Moses was with Jesus on the mount of Transfiguration. This is quite significant because Moses desired to see the glory of God in the days of Exodus when he led Israel out of Egypt to Canaan.

> *Exodus 33:13 Now therefore, I pray thee, if I have found grace in thy sight, shew me now thy way, that I may know thee, that I may find grace in thy sight: and consider that this nation is thy people.*

> *Exodus 33:18 And he said, I beseech thee, shew me thy glory.*

He wanted to know God and see His glory. This reminds me of Paul's words in Philippians when he wrote, "That I might know him…"

Moses knew he would know God by seeing God's glory.

> *Exodus 33:23 And I will take away mine hand, and thou shalt see my back parts: but my face shall not be seen.*

> *Exodus 34:29 And it came to pass, when Moses came down from mount Sinai with the two tables of testimony in Moses' hand, when he came down from the mount, that* **Moses wist not that the skin of his face shone while he talked with him.**

Moses' face shone just like Jesus' face shone! We can shine like the Lord as well, though not literally but very much so spiritually.

SHINING IN KINGDOM GLORY

2 Peter 1:19 We have also a more sure word of prophecy; whereunto ye do well that ye take heed, as unto a light that shineth in a dark place, **until the day dawn, and the day star arise in your hearts:**

We will be transformed like Jesus was when we seek to truly know Him by hearing His words and doing them, so we can live on the Rock of Zion – the Kingdom of God.

The transfiguration of Jesus on the mountain foreshadowed in physical manner the spiritual experience we can know when our minds are renewed to the understanding of being living sacrifices in self-denial. Jesus spoke to Moses and Elijah about His decease when He was transformed. This reveals that our minds must be renewed with the truths of the cross in order for us to be transformed.

After Paul wrote about that, he gave these words:

Romans 12:3 For I say, through the grace given unto me, to every man that is among you, **not to think of himself more highly than he ought to think;** *but to think soberly, according as God hath dealt to every man the measure of faith.*

This deals with our minds. Do not **think** of ourselves more highly than we ought.

14

TRANSFIGURED AS JESUS WAS TRANSFIGURED

Peter said there were seven things that must be added to our faith so that we will never fall. They are all associated with self denial and carrying our crosses. Seven is the number that is always associated with completeness.

> *1 Peter 1:5 And beside this, giving all diligence, add to your faith virtue; and to virtue knowledge; And to knowledge temperance; and to temperance patience; and to patience godliness; And to godliness brotherly kindness; and to brotherly kindness charity. For if these things be in you, and abound, they make you that ye shall neither be barren nor unfruitful in the knowledge of our Lord Jesus Christ. But he that lacketh these things is blind, and cannot see afar off, and hath forgotten that he was purged from his old sins. Wherefore the rather, brethren, give diligence to make your calling and election sure: for if ye do these things, ye shall never fall:*

Add these seven things to your faith and you shall never fall. See how these go together?

Obviously Jesus' sayings must agree with adding seven things to our faith, since He said His words cause us to not fall and Peter said these seven things will cause us to never fall.

TRANSFIGURED AS JESUS WAS TRANSFIGURED

Here is what we must add to our faith:

> Virtue
> Knowledge
> Temperance
> Patience
> Godliness
> Brotherly kindness
> Charity.

VIRTUE

Virtue is courage and manliness or valour. A backbone.

Many people know Jesus is Lord but have no backbone to live a life that stands up for Him. Such people are intimidated about being mocked by a world that mocks Christ.

Our *self* would much rather remain silent and not make waves with our friends and family, than stand for Jesus for what is right in a world where what is right is ridiculed. So, self must be denied in order to have virtue.

KNOWLEDGE

Knowledge is wisdom that makes us mature believers. We need to **learn** the things of God. Peter says grace and peace are multiplied through the **knowledge** of God. Many today do not want to learn anything if it takes more than two minutes to study. This leaves us with many believers who say Jesus is Lord, but hardly know anything about the things of God.

The devil really got an inroad when TV came along since it has turned a vast number of people into the sort that does not like to read and study. They want to see moving pictures!

Temperance

Temperance is defined as not allowing the *animal part* of us to rule us. It limits all earthly pleasures in our lives. Denying ourselves really comes into play here! Do not give in to your flesh every time your flesh wants to sin. We want to sin since it makes our flesh feel good. All sin makes the flesh feel good. But we have to curb it.

Patience

Patience is being able to sustain our Christianity and strength in the midst of tribulations and trials. More cross! Our flesh likes to "lose it" instead of believing that God is in control and everything is going to be alright, although it may take time for things to turn around.

Godliness

Godliness is true love for God and great respect for God. Respect for God means you do what He wants despite your feelings to enjoy sin. This again clearly falls under the category of denying self.

Brotherly Kindness

Charity

Brotherly kindness and charity speak for themselves.

Sometimes self wants everyone to bow down to us, but we need to deny self and bless others. If these things are not added to our faith, we will fall and never enter the eternal Kingdom!

Recall that Jesus said the man who hears his words and does them is in a house on the rock that storms cannot bring down. Add these seven things to your faith. What is our faith? It is faith that Jesus is Lord. We must have more than an understanding of who Jesus is. Our lives must be lived in accordance to who He is. If He is Lord, then we must obey His teachings. When we add these things to our recognition of Who He is, we will never fall!

Recall in our last chapter that it was Peter who wrote about our need to take special heed to the words he taught. It was this very man who had a problem hearing Christ's words. Peter did not want to hear about the cross. He did not want Jesus to go to Jerusalem and suffer and die. Peter totally missed the words about the resurrection that would follow Jesus' death.

We learned that Jesus spoke to Moses and Elijah, who suddenly appeared with Jesus on the mountain of transfiguration, about his decease, or the death He should accomplish at Jerusalem.

> *Luke 9:30-31 And, behold, there talked with him two men, which were Moses and Elias: Who appeared in glory, and spake of his decease which he should accomplish at Jerusalem.*

STARING AT LIGHT UNTIL WE SHINE

Peter's words in his second epistle referenced us to the time when the Father announced that Jesus was His Son. Peter then wrote about the light shining upon us.

> *2 Peter 1:19 We have also a more sure word of prophecy; whereunto ye do well that ye take heed, as unto a light that shineth in a dark place, until the day dawn, and the day star arise in your hearts:*

When you carefully make sure you receive what Peter was taught and endeavour to obey it, it is like looking at Light until the darkness inside you is blasted away by that Light. We then experience the sunshine beaming out from within our very beings! Jesus;' face shone like the sun. Peter said the day dawns.

You cannot have the dawning of a day without the sun. In other words, the very light we behold transforms us until we begin shining forth that same light from our own lives! And we stand and never fall.

Peter ends his 2nd Epistle with these words among others:

> *2 Peter 3:17 Ye therefore, beloved, seeing ye* **know these things** *before, beware* **lest ye** *also, being led away with the error of the wicked,* **fall from your own stedfastness.**

Jesus is Truth!

> *John 14:6 Jesus saith unto him, I am the way, the truth, and the life: no man cometh unto the Father, but by me.*

God is light.

> *1 John 1:5 This then is the message which we have heard of him, and declare unto you, that* **God is light, and in him is no darkness at all.**

> *Revelation 21:23 And the city had no need of the sun, neither of the moon, to shine in it: for* **the glory of God did lighten it, and the Lamb is the light thereof.**

John's words in Revelation mean that God is like the sun, and Jesus, Who is God manifested in flesh, is **the beams of light from that sun.**

> *2 Peter 1:4 Whereby are given unto us exceeding great and precious promises: that by these ye might be partakers of the divine nature, having escaped the corruption that is in the world through lust*

Just as the picture of hearing the **Light** of truth until it shines so much on you that you absorb it and start shining your-

TRANSFIGURED AS JESUS WAS TRANSFIGURED

self, Peter said these promises cause us to be partakers of His divine nature.

It is not **our goodness** that shines out – but His! It is His divine nature that shines out.

We did not become good by making ourselves try our human best, but we absorbed His truth into our lives and it changed us and God began shining out of us, Himself!

Paul actually wrote of the same thing.

> *2 Corinthians 3:18 But we all, with open face beholding as in a glass the glory of the Lord, are* **changed** *(META-MORPHOO) into the same image from glory to glory, even as by the Spirit of the Lord.*

> *2 Corinthians 4:5-6 For we preach not ourselves, but Christ Jesus the Lord; and ourselves your servants for Jesus' sake. (6) For God, who commanded the light to shine out of darkness, hath shined in our hearts, to give the light of the knowledge of the glory of God in the face of Jesus Christ.*

> *Romans 12:2 And be not conformed to this world: but be ye* **transformed** *(METAMORPHOO) by the renewing of your mind, that ye may prove what is that good, and acceptable, and perfect, will of God.*

> *Matthew 17:2 And was* **transfigured** *(META-MORPH-OO) before them: and his face did shine as the sun, and his raiment was white as the light.*

Paul even said that His message he preached was Jesus! In other words, his preaching of truth was like light when He preached Jesus!

Our callings and elections are made firm and sure by adding to our faith of who Jesus is. When we add the teachings of self denial and truth of the cross, we come more and more into the image of Jesus Christ!

THE LIGHT OF THE TRUTH OF THE CROSS ESTABLISHES US

When He shone like the sun as He spoke about His decease at Jerusalem, the picture was representing the light of the Truth of the cross shining in our hearts when we open our hearts for this truth and do not reject it.

> *2 Peter 1:3 According as his divine power hath given unto us all things that pertain unto life and godliness, through the knowledge of him that* **hath called us to glory and virtue:**

He called us to glory – to shine – and it provides us with everything that has to do with life and godliness. It comes through *the knowledge of Him* – through hearing His words and obeying them. All of this puts our house on the rock.

This raises another angle of the same picture. When we get these things into our hearts and we are changed into His image we shine. That is putting us on the rock. The more we are changed into His image, the more solid our houses become.

This is the fulfillment of "Thy Kingdom come."

THY WILL BE DONE, NOT OURS

When we are on the Rock, we are on Mount Zion, the Kingdom of our God. The Lord told us to pray, "Thy Kingdom come, thy will be done in earth as it is in heaven" (Matt. 6:9). In that same chapter where we read this, we also read, "Seek ye first the Kingdom of God and His righteousness..." His Kingdom is where He is King. His Kingdom is where His righteousness is accomplished. If we desire His kingdom, we must realize God's kingdom involves the things that are right, just, and all that is righteous.

Seeking His righteousness means we understand that we have to live right and according to His will in that Kingdom.

TRANSFIGURED AS JESUS WAS TRANSFIGURED

That is why so many like to call Him "Lord" but not do what He says. His Kingdom means He rules, and we live in every aspect of our lives the way He thinks we should act. We are not running this Kingdom – He is.

A person cannot have the power of the kingdom when one does not want to live the way He wants us to live. His word teaches many things that many believers like to bypass for only the fun parts.

This Kingdom is a mountain of transfiguration for our lives as well. We transfigure when we allow Jesus to speak to us, and we receive truth concerning our need to take up our crosses and denying ourselves. We change into the same image of Jesus Christ. Jesus is the daystar, or the morning star! He gives us the Daystar, and He actually is the Daystar!

Compare these verses:

> *Revelation 2:26-28 And* **he that overcometh, and keepeth my works unto the end**, *to him will I give power over the nations: And he shall rule them with a rod of iron; as the vessels of a potter shall they be broken to shivers: even as I received of my Father. And* **I will give him the morning star.**

> *2 Peter 1:19 We have also a more sure word of prophecy; whereunto ye do well that ye take heed, as unto a light that shineth in a dark place, until the day dawn,* **and the day star arise in your hearts:**

> *Revelation 22:16 I Jesus have sent mine angel to testify unto you these things in the churches.* **I am** *the root and the offspring of David, and* **the bright and morning star.**

15

THREE MEN OF THE MOUNTAINS

Malachi 4:1-6   For, behold, the day cometh, that shall burn as an oven; and all the proud, yea, and all that do wickedly, shall be stubble: and the day that cometh shall burn them up, saith the LORD of hosts, that it shall leave them neither root nor branch. But unto you that fear my name shall **the Sun of righteousness arise with healing in his wings;** *and ye shall go forth, and grow up as calves of the stall. And ye shall tread down the wicked; for they shall be ashes under the soles of your feet in the day that I shall do this, saith the LORD of hosts. Remember ye the law of* **Moses my servant**, *which I commanded unto him in Horeb for all Israel, with the statutes and judgments. Behold, I will send you* **Elijah the prophet** *before the coming of the great and dreadful day of the LORD: And he shall turn the heart of the fathers to the children, and the heart of the children to their fathers, lest I come and smite the earth with a curse.*

Malachi's 4th chapter has the same three major pictures as the account of Matthew 17's records of the mount of Transfiguration. (1) Jesus is the Sun of righteousness, with (2) Moses and (3) Elijah. While Jesus' face shone like the sun on the mountain, Elijah and Moses were also present. These three men were men *of the mountains* and did their greatest works for God on mountains! Even the cross was located on a hill called Calvary, or Golgotha.

THREE MEN OF THE MOUNTAINS

HEALING IN THE WINGS OF THE SUN

When Malachi wrote of healing from *the wings* of the sun, he actually made reference to a figure of speech regarding *beams of light* from the sun.

> *Psalm 139:9 If I take* **the wings of the morning**, *and dwell in the uttermost parts of the sea;*

The morning light comes swiftly. In the Hebrew mind, the long, dark night seemed to abruptly vanish with the fast approaching light of morning. Though today we understand that the speed of light is always the same, in the days when modern science was unknown it was understood that light seemed to fly swiftest when the morning came. The darkness was blasted away by the light in seconds after being present all night long.

Wings of the morning speak of the beams of the sun coming in so swiftly, as though one might take those swift wings and fly to the furthest reaches of the sea as quickly as possible and find that God would still be there.

Nothing moves faster than light, except God!

With that in mind, consider the light shining from Jesus' face in reference to healing. Malachi said the Sun of righteousness arises **with healing** in his wings. What might that mean?

> *2 Corinthians 4:6 For God, who commanded the light to shine out of darkness, hath shined in our hearts, to give the light of the knowledge of the glory of God in the face of Jesus Christ.*

This light is truth! He shines in our hearts to give *knowledge* of God's glory, and it heals us. In other words, it restores us. Paul wrote about light of truth shining on our hearts and said this after he mentioned Christ's glory is like light. 1 Corinthians Chapter 3 speaks of the glory of the New Covenant which we behold like in a mirror, and are changed into that same image.

Healing is returning one to health. It is restoration. We were originally created in His image, and God *heals us back* into that image by the light of the glory of Jesus.

2 Corinthians 3:18 But we all, with open face beholding as in a glass the glory of the Lord, are changed into the same image from glory to glory, even as by the Spirit of the Lord.

Peter *saw* the Rock in the revelation he received from the Father. Then Jesus proceeded to show Peter who *he* was in Christ. Jesus had not even died to have anyone baptized into His death yet, but He said **He will** build the church on the rock. Peter **will be** in Christ. Peter will share the glory of God.

MINISTRY OF LIGHT

2 Corinthians 3:7-13 But if the ministration of death, written and engraven in stones, was glorious, so that the children of Israel could not stedfastly behold the face of Moses for the glory of his countenance; which glory was to be done away: How shall not the ministration of the spirit be rather glorious? For if the ministration of condemnation be glory, much more doth the ministration of righteousness exceed in glory. For even that which was made glorious had no glory in this respect, by reason of the glory that excelleth. For if that which is done away was glorious, much more that which remaineth is glorious. Seeing then that we have such hope, we use great plainness of speech: And not as Moses, which put a vail over his face, that the children of Israel could not stedfastly look to the end of that which is abolished:

Jesus' whole ministry can be called *a ministry of light*. We must heed His ministry and His words.

Jesus explained that He brought light, but many loved darkness rather than that light (John 3:19). Those who love the light come running to it, while those who hate it run away from it to

THREE MEN OF THE MOUNTAINS

remain in darkness, lest their deeds be made manifest. When His light shone in that day, everyone was suddenly divided into two groups – those who accepted it and those who rejected it.

> *Malachi 4:4-6 Remember ye the law of Moses my servant, which I commanded unto him in Horeb for all Israel, with the statutes and judgments. Behold, I will send you Elijah the prophet before the coming of the great and dreadful day of the LORD: And he shall turn the heart of the fathers to the children, and the heart of the children to their fathers, lest I come and smite the earth with a curse.*

Moses received the Law while on Mount Sinai or Mount Horeb. Malachi even mentioned the mountain, Horeb. Elijah was also on a mountain. He turned the hearts of the children – the Israelites in his day – back to the Fathers – back to the faith of fathers Abraham, and Isaac, and Jacob.

> *1 Kings 18:17-20 And it came to pass, when Ahab saw Elijah, that Ahab said unto him, Art thou he that troubleth Israel? And he answered, I have not troubled Israel; but thou, and thy father's house, in that ye have forsaken the commandments of the LORD, and thou hast followed Baalim. Now therefore send, and gather to me all Israel* **unto mount Carmel**, *and the prophets of Baal four hundred and fifty, and the prophets of the groves four hundred, which eat at Jezebel's table. So Ahab sent unto all the children of Israel, and gathered the prophets together unto* **mount Carmel**.

Elijah called on the God of Israel in this great test of deities, and fire came down!

> *1 Kings 18:30-31 And Elijah said unto all the people, Come near unto me. And all the people came near unto him. And he repaired the altar of the LORD that was broken down.*

> *And Elijah took twelve stones, according to the number of the tribes of the sons of Jacob, unto whom the word of the LORD came, saying, Israel shall be thy name:*

He accomplished this on a mountain. We read that the prophet repaired an altar whose stones stood for the twelve tribes. This indicated the repairing of the hearts of the people who had gone astray from God into idolatry.

JACOB BECAME ISRAEL

Notice how this was written:

> *"Elijah took twelve stones, according to the number of the tribes of* **the sons of Jacob***, unto whom the word of the LORD came,* **saying, Israel shall be thy name:***"*

We read they were *sons of Jacob*. In other words, Elijah's twelve stones represented the twelve sons of a man named *Jacob*, whom God took and *changed into a different man named Israel*.

It was as though the act of repairing the stones that stood for Israel was a statement God made saying, "Now, you need to change as well. Jacob's God changed him into Israel. All of you were *Israel's sons* who have reverted to Jacob again, as though the change God effected in Jacob was reversed. You must change back into Israel again!"

> *Malachi 4:5 Behold, I will send you Elijah the prophet before the coming of the great and dreadful day of the LORD: And* **he shall turn** *the heart of the fathers to the children, and the heart of the children to their fathers, lest I come and smite the earth with a curse.*

THREE MEN OF THE MOUNTAINS

Turn, Turn, Turn

Matthew 17:10 And his disciples asked him, saying, Why then say the scribes that Elias must first come? And Jesus answered and said unto them, Elias truly shall first come, and restore all things. But I say unto you, That Elias is come already, and they knew him not, but have done unto him whatsoever they listed. Likewise shall also the Son of man suffer of them. Then the disciples understood that he spake unto them of John the Baptist.

Mark 1:4 John did baptize in the wilderness, and preach the baptism of **repentance** *for the remission of sins.*

Matthew 3:1-2 In those days came John the Baptist, preaching in the wilderness of Judaea, And saying, **Repent** *ye: for the kingdom of heaven is at hand.*

The term "repent" can also be understood as "to turn." Elijah *turned* the hearts of the children to the fathers. The fire came down as Elijah proved Jehovah was the true God, and he successfully *turned* Israel back to her former faith in God.

1 Kings 18:37-39 Hear me, O LORD, hear me, that this people may know that thou art the LORD God, **and that thou hast turned their heart back again.** *Then the fire of the LORD fell, and consumed the burnt sacrifice, and the wood, and the stones, and the dust, and licked up the water that was in the trench. And* **when all the people saw it, they fell on their faces: and they said, The LORD, he is the God; the LORD, he is the God.**

The Kingdom is a mountain of *transfiguration*. The Kingdom message *changes, or transfigures,* us into images of Jesus Christ, and we shall tread down the wicked as a result. It is a Kingdom issue.

TRUTH MUST CHANGE OUR WAY OF THINKING

> Matthew 27:33 *And when they were come unto a place called* **Golgotha, that is to say, a place of a skull,**
>
> Romans 12:1-2 *I beseech you therefore, brethren, by the mercies of God, that ye present your bodies a living sacrifice, holy, acceptable unto God, which is your reasonable service. And be not conformed to this world: but* **be ye transformed by the renewing of your mind,** *that ye may prove what is that good, and acceptable, and perfect, will of God.*

The truth of the cross and our need for self-denial must be received in our *minds*, the place of the skull. We must lose our old, selfish psyche – the way of always thinking first of self. This renders us as living sacrifices that the Kingdom requires.

Jesus was shown to be the Christ, the Son of the living God. The reference to the "living God" stresses the *eternality* of God – a life that is more powerful than death and always lives.

The gates of hell that cannot prevail are literally gates of the grave and death. Death and the grave could be no more polar opposites to the concept of the Living God than they are.

In another instance, Jesus was challenged by the devil's use of the high priest in Matthew 26. What Jesus said, and the way Caiaphas appealed to Him to speak, caused hell to tremble.

> Matthew 26:63-66 *But Jesus held his peace. And the high priest answered and said unto him,* **I adjure thee by the living God,** *that thou tell us whether thou be* **the Christ, the Son of God. Jesus saith unto him, Thou hast said:** *nevertheless I say unto you, Hereafter shall ye see the Son of man sitting on the right hand of power, and coming in the clouds of heaven. Then the high priest rent his clothes, saying, He hath spoken blasphemy; what further need have we*

of witnesses? behold, now ye have heard his blasphemy. What think ye? They answered and said, He is guilty of death.

THE CONFESSION OF THE ROCK

The *confession of the Rock* declares Jesus is the Son of the Living God. This means that eternal life is in the very bosom of Jesus Christ. Hell hates the very thought of it! The gates of hell are the gates of death and the grave and death is challenged and threatened by this declaration. Not only did Jesus affirm association with eternal life, but when He proclaimed He would build His Church on the Rock, He implied that the Church partakes of this eternal life and divine nature as well.

This lone statement caused Caiaphas to quake and demand Christ's death. Whenever death hears a *mortal* man speak of faith in the *Living* God, it says **kill** that one and prove him wrong!

But Jesus said the gates of death shall not prevail! The Son of the living God will indeed resurrect! This promise is given *to us* as well, if we take up our crosses and follow Jesus. Our crucifixions with the Lord will see us suffer the denial of self so that the power of resurrection can reside in our souls. Peter's confession of the Father's revelation was a very profound statement!

Hell does not mind if you believe Jesus was a good teacher. It does not even mind if you believe Jesus was a Son in the sense that there were others before Him who were sons as much as He was. In fact, you can even affirm that Jesus is Lord. But when you state and totally believe that Jesus is the Son of the Living God, and that you will follow His words and obey His lordship, you have challenged all of death. All that is opposed to God becomes your enemy.

Peter himself said that the Lord is building up a structure on a rock, and this structure is made of many living stones.

1 Peter 2:5-7 Ye also, as lively stones, are built up a spiritual house, an holy priesthood, to offer up spiritual sacrifices, acceptable to God by Jesus Christ. Wherefore also it is contained in the scripture, Behold, I lay in Sion a chief corner stone, elect, precious: and he that believeth on him shall not be confounded. Unto you therefore which believe he is precious: but unto them which be disobedient, the stone which the builders disallowed, the same is made the head of the corner,

John said this confession is what gives eternal life.

1 John 4:15 Whosoever shall confess that Jesus is the Son of God, God dwelleth in him, and he in God.

1 John 5:5 Who is he that overcometh the world, but he that believeth that Jesus is the Son of God?

1 John 5:20 And we know that the Son of God is come, and hath given us an understanding, that we may know him that is true, and we are in him that is true, [even] in his Son Jesus Christ. This is the true God, and eternal life.

The house on the Rock stands boldly and firm against the face of death. This house cannot be thrown down by death's attempts. But the house on sand – the souls who call Jesus "Lord" but never obey His words of self-denial, cannot withstand the attacks of death. Because they would not taste the death of self-denial in taking up their crosses, they unfortunately taste death when storms attack, and it is then that they will permanently lose their lives never to rise again.

Moses and Elijah appeared with Jesus on the mountain of Transfiguration. This mountain speaks of the Kingdom. Jesus told us to seek first God's Kingdom and God's righteousness (Matt. 6:33). That righteousness shines like the sun upon us – the Sun of righteousness – and, in turn, makes us righteous!

Malachi's 4th chapter begins with words about the proud who do not deny self whatsoever, and are burnt and destroyed as a result. The righteous, on the other hand, are as calves of the stall, and not only remain alive and well, but grow and are nurtured.

Elijah and Moses are mentioned in all of this. Everything here connects us with the mountain of Transfiguration – the mountain of *transformation and change*. We read about the Sun of righteousness, Moses and Elijah, as well as the note about the righteous who will stand and go on to grow like calves of the stall, while others fall and die.

Hosea 4:6 My people are destroyed for lack of knowledge...

How important it is for us to learn the truth and come to correct knowledge! If people are destroyed for lack of knowledge, what does that say for those who obtain it?

Jesus fought the battle as the Captain of our salvation on the cross. Though He died like a lamb of sacrifice, He achieved the victory of a Lion! That little lamb conquered death – the very power of the devil, himself.

16

BACK ON THE KINGDOM MOUNTAIN IN EDEN

> *Ezekiel 28:13-14 Thou hast been in **Eden the Garden of God**; every precious stone was thy covering, the sardius, topaz, and the diamond, the beryl, the onyx, and the jasper, the sapphire, the emerald, and the carbuncle, and gold: the workmanship of thy tabrets and of thy pipes was prepared in thee in the day that thou wast created. Thou art the anointed cherub that covereth; and I have set thee so: thou wast upon **the holy mountain of God**; thou hast walked up and down in the midst of the stones of fire.*

From a description of the King of Tyrus, which some believe may refer to satan's prefall existence, we see a remarkable reference to some details of the Garden in Eden that are not noted in Genesis. We read of three distinct *sections* related to the Garden: Eden, the Garden and the holy mountain of God.

In Volume I we noted how Genesis 2 shows that Eden was not the Garden, but the Garden was *in* the eastern region of the larger district of Eden. In Ezekiel we read an additional detail. There was a *holy mountain of God* in the Garden. It's as though the Edenic picture is patterned in the Temple. First, there is the Outer, larger Court of the district of Eden. Then there is the Holy Place of the Garden, and finally the Most Holy Place called the Holy Mountain of God. Formerly, we noted that the Garden *was* the Most Holy Place, with its entrance barred by cherubim just as the Most Holy Place was barred by a veil with cherubim embroidered into it.. However, the information provided in Ezekiel 28 seems to suggest that deeper inside the Garden was this Holy Mountain of God that would more correctly correspond to the Most Holy Place. May the Lord continue to refine our understanding.

Jesus spoke of the House on the Rock *that would not fall*. With the added picture of a Holy Mountain in the Garden, we can now see an even greater picture that relates our present Kingdom position in Christ to the *fall of Adam and Eve*. Adam was on this Holy Mountain and fell, so to speak. He lost his position there. The correspondence of the Garden Mountain and Christ's House on the Rock shows us that the Kingdom of Jesus Christ, the Last Man Adam, is indeed a restoration of the lost Garden Kingdom.

To think that we can heed the revelation from Jesus Christ concerning the truths of cross and self denial so as to never fall! What an incredibly wonderful promise in light of Adam's fall from the Garden Kingdom. Satan managed to cause Adam to fall from that Rock, the Holy Mountain of God, and out of the Garden completely. He deposed King Adam. But the child of God who denies self and takes up his/her cross to follow the Lord cannot fall! Satan is only able to appeal to the carnality of fleshly lusts of our lives. If we deny ourselves, we are actually robbing satan of any manner by which he can appeal to us!

God made man from the dust of the ground, and cursed satan to eat the dust of the ground for food. This shows a spiritual picture of how fleshliness and carnality are the things satan feeds upon in our lives. If we receive the self-denying message of the cross and live by it, we rob satan of what he feeds upon! Like Jesus, we can say, "the prince of this world has nothing in me" (John 14:30).

The Flaming Sword at the Garden Entrance

Consider the flaming sword at the Garden entrance, and correspond that concept with the thoughts we gained from the second revelation from the Son of God regarding self denial and the cross. Jesus Christ's word is like a sharp and flaming two-edged sword. It cuts away carnality because it is the truth of the cross and self denial. When we hear His words and do them, like a wise man building his house on a rock, we experience a *transformation*. This transformation makes us so that we do not fall. I do not speak as though we lose the potential to fall, for the moment we cease living this life of self-denial and "walking in the Spirit" is the moment we fall (Galatians 5:16)! The renewing of our minds occurs, and self denial becomes a way of thinking. The revelation from the Son of God that follows the revelation of Christ's identity from the Father is the sword that removes carnality and fleshliness from our lives.

What can the devil appeal to if we have denied ourselves and fully received the truth of the cross and live it? No wonder Peter said we'd never fall if we go beyond faith and add to our faith the seven elements of holiness! Adam and Eve fell due to the self focus the devil managed to tempt them to experience. If we take up our crosses and live lives of self denial, we will enter the Kingdom Mountain of God and rule and reign with Jesus and never fall as Adam fell!

Jesus played out an *object lesson* in Matthew 17 on the Mount of Transfiguration. The revelation of the cross that He taught the disciples in Matthew 16, one chapter earlier, was depicted in a *living parable*, so to speak, when He took them on that Rock. Elijah and Moses spoke with Him about the decease He should experience at Jerusalem. Once again, Peter did not want to hear about that, and suggested they all remain there with three Tabernacles. The Father once again gave the first revelation of Christ's identity, and reminded Peter to receive the Son's revelation: "This is my beloved Son in whom I am well pleased. Hear ye Him."

BACK ON THE KINGDOM MOUNTAIN IN EDEN

When Jesus was transfigured that day, His face was said to shine like the sun. There is one other New Testament reference that mentions this same picture.

> *Revelation 1:16 And he had in his right hand seven stars: and out of his mouth went a sharp twoedged sword: and his countenance was as the sun shineth in his strength.*

With His face shining like the sun as it did on the holy mountain, we read of another striking picture that ties all these thoughts together. A two-edged sword came forth from his mouth. This displays two connecting pictures to the restored Garden Kingdom of which we are studying. His face shone on the Kingdom Mountain of Transfiguration that corresponds to the Holy Mountain of God in the Garden. The sword coming from His mouth corresponds to the flaming sword placed at the Garden entrance that turned every way.

When Jesus' face shone like the sun on the mountain, we saw a picture emphasizing transfiguration, or change and transformation. It represented the light of the knowledge of the glory of God in Jesus' face (2 Corinthians 4:6) that changes us into His same image from glory to glory (2 Corinthians 3:18). The message of the cross and self denial is that transfiguring message.

LIVING SACRIFICES & THE WILL OF THE FATHER

> *Romans 12:1-2 I beseech you therefore, brethren, by the mercies of God, that ye present your bodies a living sacrifice, holy, acceptable unto God, which is your reasonable service. And be not conformed to this world: but be ye transformed by the renewing of your mind, that ye may prove what is that good, and acceptable, and perfect, will of God.*

Jesus said only those who do the will of His Father shall enter into the Kingdom (Matthew 7:21). Such will have houses on the rock that will not fall. Paul mentioned the "perfect will of

God" as well. He connected that to Christians who are living sacrifices and are transformed by the renewing of their minds. So we see a threefold focus upon this overall Kingdom picture. There in Romans 12 is (1) the self denial of the cross in being living sacrifices, (2) the transformation/transfiguration, (3) and the will of the Father. All of which are required to enter the Kingdom.

How would you like to be on the Holy Kingdom Mountain of God in the Garden where satan cannot cause you to fall as he caused Adam and Eve to fall? The New Testament not only restores us to the prefall existence of Adam in the Garden Kingdom, but it reveals to us the great revelation from the Son of God as to how to ensure we get there and never fall from that position as Adam fell.

Jesus scolded Peter and called him satan when Peter resisted the revelation of the cross. He said Peter became an offence to Him. Can we not see this in Adam as well? When Adam chose to not follow God's Word given to him, and side along with his wife, Eve, and succumb to sin, he became an offence to the cause of God. Those who stumble at the stumblingstone of the offence of the cross become an offence themselves, and cannot *stand* in the Kingdom. Such will not enter the Kingdom. They may know Jesus' identity as Lord, but they do not actually act as though He is Lord due to their unwillingness to do what He says.

SHINING ONCE AGAIN IN THE GARDEN KINGDOM

Some believe Adam literally shone with glory before his fall. They claim the reason Adam and Eve were naked and knew it not was because the glory of God upon their lives caused them to not see their nakedness (Genesis 2:25). If this be the case, is it not a wonderful thought that our willingness to receive the revelation of self denial is like beholding a light that shines in a dark place? It shines upon us until the day dawns, and the day star arises and shines out from within our hearts (2 Peter 1:19). We are transfigured to shine like the Lord once again in the Garden Kingdom!

YOUR THINKING FIRST AND THEN YOUR BODY

God's Spirit resides within the true believer. The revelation from the Son concerning the cross removes the carnality and fleshliness that hinders this Spirit with us from operating through us in Kingdom power. Doubts, unbelief, and self-exaltation that carnality produces in our hearts are cut away by the flaming sword of Christ's revelation! When we rid our lives of this hindering factor of unbelief, we will go forth as believers with miracle-working faith! They hinder God's power in us from manifesting.

Paul's words in Romans 12 about presenting *our bodies* as living sacrifices and renewing *our minds* are in perfect accord with his previous words in the same Book of Romans.

> *Romans 6:13 Neither yield ye your members as instruments of unrighteousness unto sin: but* **yield yourselves unto God***, as those that are alive from the dead,* **and your members** *as instruments of righteousness unto God.*

Paul shows two stages here. First, we yield *ourselves* to God. Secondly, we yield our *bodily members* to God. First, *our minds* must be renewed by reckoning that we are dead indeed unto sin, and alive unto God through Christ (Romans 6:11). You cannot be alive to God unless you died to sin. When Romans 6:13 tells us to present ourselves as those who are alive from the dead, it is telling us to get a revelation that we really did die to sin with Christ so we could see ourselves as those alive unto God.

The house on the Rock receives the qualities of the Rock upon which it is built. Jesus died to sin once, and is now alive unto God (Romans 6:10). Unless we realize we actually died to sin with Him (Romans 6:6), and know that sin does not have dominion over us any more (Romans 6:14), we cannot really yield ourselves as those who are *alive to God*. Yielding ourselves as those who are alive to God means we come to God fully knowing and believing *we* are dead to sin and alive to Him, and we *expect* His power to kick into effect in our lives and empower us to do miraculous things for the Kingdom. We must consciously appreciate what it is to say we are alive to God. Many know the Bible teaches this, but do not consciously "get it".

It's like saying, "I get it now, Lord! I receive your revelation! I died to sin *with* you, and that means I am also alive from the dead *with* you. You are the Rock, and You died and arose again in resurrection power. I am like a house built on this Rock. Your qualities are transferred to me, and I can say I therefore died and rose again, and have Your resurrection power on my life. Knowing this, I hereby present my body to God for His use as a set of instruments of righteousness. I expect in faith for Your power to manifest in me and empower me to physically accomplish Your will in this world. Come Kingdom of God! Be done, will of God!"

When we present *ourselves* to God, we see emphasis upon the way we *think*, or reckon. Our minds *know* that we were crucified with Christ (Gal. 2:20), so we take up our crosses and live a crucified life, or a life of *living sacrifice*. We renew our minds, and our bodies are rendered living sacrifices for His righteous use.

See the progression? We get our *minds* renewed to the concept of the cross by "hearing these sayings" (Matthew 7:24) of Jesus, knowing we are crucified with Christ. Then we *live* this concept in our very *bodies* and "do them" as we offer our bodily members as instruments of His righteousness and expect Him to empower us as a result.

We must first *know* this truth by having received this revelation from the Son, and present *ourselves* as those alive from the dead. Then we *do* what He gave us in revelation by living a self-denying life where our bodily members are no longer our own, but are rendered to God as instruments for Him to use in *righteous deeds*.

The truths of self-denial and carrying our crosses transform us by renewing our minds. The sword of the truth of His words cuts away proud and self-exalting attitudes. It removes the self-centredness that caused Adam to fall in the Garden. We are taught how we are crucified with Christ and shown how we must live lives that are conducive to that fact. This truth slashes away in every direction like a flaming sword. It misses nothing in our lives, for it turns every way. Removing these carnal traits causes us to be able to withstand storms from the gates of hell, and remain standing.

THE GATES OF HELL SHALL NOT PREVAIL

Adam was told he would die should he eat of the forbidden fruit. When he indeed did sin, he was informed he would return to the dust of the ground. In other words, the gates of the *grave* prevailed against Adam. Death and the grave are the meanings of the term "hell" or "hades" (Matt. 16:18).

If we *take up our crosses* by receiving the revelation of self-denial and thereby renew our minds, and *deny ourselves* by offering our bodily members for God to use as His instruments, we lose our lives to find them again! This is resurrection power. Finding a life you lost is called resurrection. This means the gates of "death and the grave" cannot prevail against us as they prevailed against Adam and saw him die. Adam not only fell from the Garden's Kingdom Mountain, but he also fell into death and the grave.

17

IT IS ENOUGH:
WHEN THE SWORD STOPS

Genesis 3:24 So he drove out the man; and he placed at the east of the Garden of Eden Cherubims, and a flaming sword which turned every way, to keep the way of the Tree of Life.

Genesis 22:10-12 And Abraham stretched forth his hand, and took the knife to slay his son. And the angel of the LORD called unto him out of heaven, and said, Abraham, Abraham: and he said, Here am I. And he said, Lay not thine hand upon the lad, neither do thou any thing unto him: for now I know that thou fearest God, seeing thou hast not withheld thy son, thine only son from me.

Abraham's faith was strong when God told him to take Isaac and offer him upon Mount Moriah. He knew that God promised he would be the father of many nations. But Isaac had not begotten any children as of yet. Abraham knew Isaac would have to resurrect if he slew the boy in order for God's promise to be true and come to pass. If you read the passage carefully, you will find that the book of Hebrews pointed out this very truth.

Hebrews 11:17-19 By faith Abraham, when he was tried, offered up Isaac: and he that had received the promises offered up his only begotten son, **Of whom it was said, That**

IT IS ENOUGH – WHEN THE SWORD STOPS

> *in Isaac shall thy seed be called:* Accounting that God was able to raise him up, even from the dead; from whence also he received him in a figure.

The writer of Hebrews specifically noted that Isaac would be the person through whom Abraham's seed would be called. Why say that if God wanted to see Isaac dead? Here we see an indication of what Abraham kept in his heart during that awful ordeal.

Believing God to that kind of extent requires self-denial. Imagine Abraham's greatest promise from God being threatened by the thought of taking Isaac's life. How could he be the father of many nations if his only son was slain through whom God said this would be fulfilled? But Abraham's faith in God's word that said he would be the father of many nations through Isaac overcame any selfish temptation to preserve that promise in his own power.

Once God saw that Abraham's faith was strong, He commanded the knife to stop. It seems the command for him to not bring the knife down upon Isaac was actually a word regarding the sword that was cutting away *Abraham's* flesh. Abraham had so much faith that he was truly a doer of that Word and not a hearer only. The sword need not cut any further.

Abraham took *three days* to arrive at Mount Moriah where he offered Isaac on the altar. The duration of three days in the Bible always implies a truth about resurrection power through the work of the cross, for Christ's resurrection occurred three days after He was crucified. We could, therefore, say that Abraham overcame the threat and challenge of death by *third-day resurrection power!*

The sword at the Garden entrance is meant to slice away unbelief and doubt that hinders us from entering that rest. (Heb. 4:1-3). When the cutting has accomplished enough and has succeeded in removing the unbelief that holds us out, God says, "It is enough."

COUNTING ON THE FLESH

Satan tempted David to number Israel (1 Chronicles 21). The temptation was rooted in a desire to literally *count on the flesh* rather than have faith in the power of God that was with Israel. Mosaic Law stated that whenever a census of the population was taken, an atonement cost was required at ½ shekel per each person over twenty years of age (Exodus 30:12-15). It was a reminder that Israel was God's possession whom He ransomed with the price of atonement sacrifice.

A ransom had to occur in order for Israel to be God's people. Without that sacrifice, Israel was nothing. They were already ransomed by the Lord since Egypt's Exodus (Exodus 15:13), but this atonement payment served as a reminder to them of this fact every time they were to be numbered ever since.

David counted the population of Israel without the required atonement cost from each person, thereby acting as though he was *counting on the flesh*. He disregarded the fact that Israel was God's people, and regardless of how large or how small the nation was, God's power would sustain them. They need not look to their own human might when considering how successful they might be as a nation in the face of foes and enemies. Basically, David acted in unbelief that God would keep them safe.

We do this all the time when we face trials and troubles of life. Such a mindset hinders us from experiencing Kingdom living. In fact, God refuses to allow such people to enter His Kingdom. The sword of his Word demanding self denial keeps them out.

We must never look to our fleshly might in order to determine how we will fare in life's battles. God is with us. However, David yielded to the temptation to deal with everything through natural and fleshly power.

Joab rebuked the king and informed him that he personally wished Israel was one hundred times bigger than she was. But to bring God's wrath upon the nation by assessing their strength

IT IS ENOUGH – WHEN THE SWORD STOPS

while disregarding the atonement ransom was certainly not the solution.

The prophet Gad went to David and informed him that God was angry and would punish Israel for his sin. David had three choices. (1) Accept a means of punishment wherein God would afflict the land with three years of famine, (2) three months of fleeing before enemy nations in defeat, or (3) three days of direct plaguing of the nation by God, Himself. David chose to fall into God's hands and accept the three days of plague.

Notice the emphasis in both Abraham's experience and David's with a three day period (Gen. 22:4; 1 Chron. 21:12).

Three days passed, and pestilence swept across the land slaying thousands. David went atop Mount Moriah where Abraham had offered Isaac on a third day, and saw an angel suspended between the earth and the sky with a sword drawn in his hand over the city Jerusalem (2 Chron. 21:15-16). The king cried to God, and suddenly grasped the value of atonement that he formerly shirked in numbering Israel without the ransom money. He asked God to afflict him and his household, sparing Jerusalem, for it was his sin and not theirs that brought on the devastation. David called Israel the sheep, and like a true shepherd who gives his life for the sheep (John 10:11) he offered himself for them instead. Having his death count as the deaths of the people is the very principle of atonement sacrifice.

On that third day, God told the angel with the sword "It is enough!" (1 Chron. 21:15) David came to the same mountain where Abraham offered Isaac on another third day. The king denied himself so fully that one could say that enough cutting by the sword of self-denial had occurred. As with Abraham, the knife was ready to slay another, but in truth, the sword had been cutting deeply into David's soul separating fleshliness from his heart so as to leave a self-denying man of God. Being a kind of image of Christ, God described David as a man after His own heart.

"Moriah" literally means "seen of God" or "what God causes one to see." Moriah was truly a mountain of third-day, Kingdom *revelation*. God had caused Abraham and David to see a revelation of self-denial – the sword at the Garden Kingdom entrance. Jesus said, "Upon this rock (mountain) I will build my church, and the gates of hell shall not prevail against it" (Matthew 16:18). Self will have been so removed from those who climb upon this mountain that satan has nothing in them to defeat. Death, the only power the devil ever had, was defeated in the hearts of these men of self-denial. The crosses they carried removed all self life that death could afflict.

The lesson to be learned is that the revelation of Jesus Christ regarding the cross of self denial must be taken and borne. It delivers us, like a sharp two-edged sword, from all fleshly unbelief and self-centredness.

Both David and Abraham went atop Moriah and built altars of sacrifice. Both experienced a blade ready to slay, and saw the knife stop. Both men committed acts of selflessness that foreshadowed the great Atonement and selfless sacrifice of Jesus Christ for our salvation! When we venture forth straight into the flaming sword of Christ's Word of self-denial, the sword will slice and cut away all unbelief and self-focus, and leave us as images of Jesus Christ back in the Garden Kingdom!

As the Ark of Covenant bore two golden cherubim on its Mercy Seat, God placed (literally "Tabernacle") cherubim at the entrance of the Garden around the flaming sword. God spoke from between the cherubim during the days of the Exodus (Exodus 25:22). Similarly, the sword of the Word was between the cherubim in Eden. Being the focal object of the Atonement ritual each year, the Ark of the Covenant has God's Word of atonement going forth. Abraham and David both caught this revelation of atonement on Mount Moriah where Solomon later placed the Ark of the Covenant in the Temple.

Abraham and David! What great men of God! No wonder the very first verse in the entire New Testament reads as follows:

IT IS ENOUGH – WHEN THE SWORD STOPS

Matthew 1:1 The book of the generation of Jesus Christ, **the son of David, the son of Abraham.**

18

MEASURING THE SPIRIT RIVER OF LIFE

The Spirit of God is compared to a River of Life in Scripture. As we have noted, there was a River of Life in Eden as well as the Tree of Life. There was both drink and food.

Ezekiel saw the vision of this River as did John the revelator. Both men saw the River with the Tree of Life on either side with leaves for healing and fruit for food.

> *Ezekiel 47:12 And by the river upon the bank thereof, on this side and on that side, shall grow all trees for meat, whose leaf shall not fade, neither shall the fruit thereof be consumed: it shall bring forth new fruit according to his months, because their waters they issued out of the sanctuary: and the fruit thereof shall be for meat, and the leaf thereof for medicine.*

> *Revelation 22:1-2 And he shewed me a pure river of water of life, clear as crystal, proceeding out of the throne of God and of the Lamb. In the midst of the street of it, and on either side of the river, was there the Tree of Life, which bare twelve manner of fruits, and yielded her fruit every month: and the leaves of the tree were for the healing of the nations.*

The only difference is that Ezekiel saw it coming from the Temple and John saw it coming from the throne of God and the

MEASURING THE SPIRIT RIVER OF LIFE

Lamb. But the fact is that God and the Lamb are the Temple. So, Ezekiel and John actually saw the same thing!

Revelation 21:22 And I saw no Temple therein: for the Lord God Almighty and the Lamb are the Temple of it.

When Ezekiel saw the river flow from the Temple, it flowed towards the east (Ezek. 47:1). Ezekiel was directed to walk away from the Temple with the river's current and was specifically shown how far he should walk. A man with a measuring line measured one thousand cubits. Ezekiel was told to walk that distance in the river, and when he did the water arose *to the level of his ankles*.

This happened two more times. The second thousand cubits took him into water up to his knees and then at the three thousand cubit mark the water was up to his loins. One more measurement of another thousand cubits led Ezekiel into waters in which he swam.

Ezekiel 47:3-5 And when the man that had the line in his hand went forth eastward, he measured a thousand cubits, and he brought me through the waters; the waters were to the **ankles**. *Again he measured a thousand, and brought me through the waters; the waters were to the* **knees**. *Again he measured a thousand, and brought me through; the waters were to the* **loins**. *Afterward he measured a thousand; and it was a river that I could not pass over: for the waters were risen, waters to swim in, a river that could not be passed over.*

There is spiritual significance to the three levels of ankle-deep, knee-deep and waist-deep water. The overall picture of these three levels of water and trees with fruit and leaves are likewise found in the First Psalm!

Psalms 1:1-3 Blessed is the man that **walketh** *not in the counsel of the ungodly, nor* **standeth** *in the way of sinners,* *nor **sitteth** in the seat of the scornful. But his delight is in the law of the LORD; and in his law doth he meditate day and night. And he shall be like a tree planted by the rivers of water, that bringeth forth his fruit in his season; his leaf also shall not wither; and whatsoever he doeth shall prosper.*

Note the three elements of walking, standing and sitting. Then we read such a person who follows his directive shall be like the trees Ezekiel and John saw on either side of the river of Life. We specifically read of ***leaves*** that will not wither and ***fruit*** that does not lack, just as Ezekiel and John were shown trees whose ***leaves*** are for healing and ***fruit*** for meat. Thank the Lord that the leaves do not wither, for if they are for healing this means that there shall always be healing!

WHAT ARE LEAVES AND FRUIT?

While driving in California through an orange orchard, the leaves and fruit of the Tree of Life (Rev. 22) came to my mind as I looked at all the orange-laden trees. What is the identity of the leaves of the Tree of Life, since it seemed obvious the fruit of Life stood as the fruit of the Spirit in a believer's life?

Then it hit me! If the fruit are the fruit of the Spirit, and the leaves are for ***healing***, the leaves stand for the gifts of the Spirit, such as gifts of healing (1 Cor. 12:9)! I long considered how it was always God's will for every believer to manifest much fruit and many gifts of the Spirit! Though gifts alone are not sufficient (remember Matt. 7:22), the fruit of love combined with the gifts of the Spirit provide a healthy and much needed ministry that is not just sounding brass and tinkling cymbals. When only the gifts operate with no fruit (compare 1 Cor. 13:1 and Gal. 5:22), we have a very unbalanced Christian life.

David said that the people who refuse to walk in the counsel of the ungodly, stand in the way of sinners and sit in the seat of the scornful will be like those trees whose leaves do not wither nor lack fruit. Obviously the key to such a life lived in the will of

MEASURING THE SPIRIT RIVER OF LIFE

God is found in the references to not walking, standing and sitting in such negative positions. If we want to be trees of Life whose leaves and fruit are bountiful, we must learn what it means to not walk, stand nor sit in the ways David described.

To walk, then stand and finally sit shows a regression. It is going from mobility to immobility. It is deterioration. Such walking is a bad walking, for it is walking in ungodly people's counsel. When we listen to the advice of ungodly people, it will not be long before we regress and begin *standing* in the way of sinners.

Standing in the way of sinners can be easily misunderstood as hindering them as they try to know God. That is not what it means. The *way of sinners* is the *lifestyle* and the *manner of living* that sinners experience. It is their pathway, so to speak. It is like saying we should not use the broad **way** that leads to destruction (Matt. 7:13) when we read to not stand in the **way** of sinners.

Jesus said that operation of gifts of the Spirit while living lives in iniquity will cause Him to *not know us* (Matt 7:21-23). Those whom he called workers of iniquity obviously were committing works of the flesh and not manifesting the fruit of the Spirit. Before He mentioned this in Matthew 7, He distinctly referred to false prophets who are known by their fruit. He also said that there is a narrow **way** which leads to life and a broad **way** which leads to destruction. Psalm 1 seems to pull all these same elements together in speaking of our need to avoid standing in *the way of sinners* in order to be trees with the desired fruit and leaves that do not wither.

THE LAW OF THE SPIRIT OF LIFE

Ezekiel's vision also explains our need to not walk, stand nor sit as David described *using a most spiritual picture!*

The River is the Spirit of God. It can be **measured** as the man with the measuring line indicated. This is because there is a **Law** of this Spirit of Life in Christ Jesus (Romans 8:2). Since it is called the **Law** of the Spirit, we are to understand that the

Spirit works in a certain manner that can be comprehended. Once we understand how the Spirit of God operates, and what circumstances are required for the Spirit's blessings, we can benefit from it! In other words, it is calculable, and measurable.

It is sad that many believers are uneducated as to how the Spirit works and what qualifies us to be recipients of His blessings, even when that Spirit dwells within them.

Notice that it is called the Spirit of Life. Jesus also spoke of the *way of Life*. We read that God's ways are above our ways, so we require education about them. To learn the in's and out's of the Law of the Spirit is to receive the mind of Christ and understand how He works. Though He was God manifest in flesh, Jesus knew in His humanity how to see the Spirit within Him empower Him to do many wonderful feats for the Kingdom. We have a responsibility to qualify ourselves for the opportunity to see the Spirit do what it indwells us to do.

CEASING TO WALK IN UNGODLY COUNSEL BECAUSE THE RIVER TOUCHES OUR ANKLES

Ezekiel's first venture into the River corresponds to the first note David mentioned. Walking is accomplished by using our *ankles*. When Ezekiel's ankles overflowed with the River we see *the influence of the Spirit* upon the parts of our lives – not literally ankles – that are influenced by ungodly counsel. If we can break any influence upon those aspects of ourselves to which ungodly counsel might appeal, we simply will not walk in such counsel.

The Spirit, like Ezekiel's river, must envelope the part of us that will walk after ungodly counsel when tempted. Our flesh can get out of hand, and the mere desire to not fulfil fleshly lusts will not stop that. We need a greater Power. That is exactly why we receive the Baptism of the Holy Ghost, the River. Following the directive of the man with the measuring line into the water to the ankles represents following the law of the Spirit that has been taught to us so that it successfully influences our "walk".

Even Jesus spoke of cutting off our hands and plucking out our eyes in order to not sin (Matt. 5:29). His words spiritually refer to this same need to deal with the parts of our lives that are influenced by sin so we cease from sin. If the Spirit touches our "walks", we will simply not walk in ungodly counsel.

ANKLES, KNEES & LOINS: MEMBERS PRESENTED TO GOD TO USE

Paul taught us to present ourselves to God as people who are alive from the dead, as well as our bodily members for His instruments of righteousness (Rom. 6:13). When we appeal to the Spirit of God by conscious prayer for Him to empower us to not sin, and then believe for Him to do that, He will respond! This kind of approach to the situation is called "walking after the Spirit" (Rom. 8:1). Attempting to stop committing sin through the use of our weak human will power does not work. Such futile effort is called "walking after the flesh". Paul described that plight by writing about possessing the will to not sin but not finding it within his flesh to do so (Rom. 7:18).

TO SERVE IN OLDNESS OF THE LETTER, OR IN NEWNESS OF THE SPIRIT

Many think Paul described the ever-present dilemma of forever wanting to stop committing sins, but resigning ourselves to the fact we will not. I do not believe that is what Paul meant. While he listed all the frustration of wanting to do what is right and failing, he happened to mention that this occurred whenever *he*, in his own frail human power, tried to do such good. That is the key to understanding the Law of the Spirit. In other words, we cannot succeed if all we do is resort to our own human effort and will power when we try to perform the will of God. Who said there was not another power to which we can appeal aside from self-effort?

Paul spoke of the same struggle in the book of Galatians and said that so long as we walk "after the Spirit" we will not fulfill the lusts of the flesh (Gal 5:16).

Before he mentioned the struggle in Romans 7, Paul stated it was not enough to know we must serve God (Rom. 7:6). He went on to say it was a matter of ***how*** we serve Him that is the issue. People think that so long as they try to serve God, regardless of how they do it, they are doing His will.

> *Romans 7:6 But now we are delivered from the law, that being dead wherein we were held; that we should serve in newness of spirit, and not in the oldness of the letter.*

We read that one has to be delivered from the Law so that one could stop serving God by the "oldness of the letter". The Law referred to the Old Testament way of living by "carnal ordinances" (Heb. 9:10) and "the power of a carnal commandment" (Heb. 7:16). As one wise minister once said, Law only showed you how dirty your face was, but did not provide you with the wash cloth, soap, and water to clean your face. Therefore, serving God in the oldness of the letter is the type of struggle Paul illustrated in Romans 7, and described in Romans 8 as "Walking after the flesh." We should instead serve God by the newness of the Spirit. Ezekiel's adventure in the River illustrates how.

Serving in oldness of the letter is basically taking a law that provides no empowerment to do what it commands. Serving in newness of the Spirit is resorting to God's Spirit to live an overcoming life. We do this by conscious prayer for Him to take our bodily members and inspire and empower us to use them for His righteousness.

After Paul listed all the atrocious failings one experiences in using will power alone to serve God (which is walking after the flesh), he asked who could deliver him from his body of death. He just remarked how sin resided in his flesh, and it was not him but that sin that forced him to do what he did not want to do. So, what other deliverance can one experience than by simply dying and being made free from that body that houses such a force called sin? But then Paul answered his own question!

> *Romans 7:24-25 O wretched man that I am! who shall deliver me from the body of this death?* **I thank God through Jesus Christ our Lord.** *So then with the mind I myself serve the law of God; but with the flesh the law of sin.*

Who would deliver Him? He said He thanked God, for God delivers! How would God deliver him? God would deliver Paul from his body of death *through Christ Jesus.* He just wrote that we are dead to the law by the body of Jesus (Rom. 7:4) so that we can start producing "fruit" unto God (there's that reference to fruit again!.)

Instead of **walking** in the counsel of the ungodly, we need to be walking a lifestyle that manifests fruit of the Spirit. Instead of **standing** in the pathway that sinners stand in, we need to live lives that show forth the glory of Jesus Christ! It is God who accomplishes that all due to our union to Jesus Christ our Lord and His death. When we realize we died with Christ to sin (Rom. 6:10) through sharing His death (Rom. 6:3), we will realize we do not have to let sin rule in our mortal bodies any longer (Rom. 6:12). This is how God delivers us through Jesus Christ.

CEASING TO STAND IN THE WAY OF SINNERS BECAUSE THE RIVER TOUCHES OUR KNEES

The parts of our bodies that assist us in standing are our **knees**. After David spoke of our need to not walk in ungodly counsel, he said we must not **stand** in the way of sinners. After Ezekiel allowed the water to immerse his ankles, the water immersed his knees. We see the identical pattern in both references.

Submersing the knees being in the River of the Spirit represents the need of the Spirit to affect those parts of our lives to which the *way of sinners* appeals. When we offer these parts of our lives to the Lord, His Spirit then makes them instruments of His righteousness, and we will find power to resist the temptation to allow these "knees" to stand in the lifestyle in which sinners stand.

CEASING TO SIT IN THE SEAT OF THE SCORNFUL BECAUSE THE RIVER TOUCHES OUR LOINS

To go from walking, to standing and finally to *sitting* in the seat of the scornful puts us in the very place where the ungodly sat who first provided us with their counsel to walk at the start of this downward slope. We then join those ungodly counsellors and begin criticizing all that is righteous after having only first *heard* counsel from the sinner, and then having stood in the lifestyle of sinners. It worsens just as the trend from walking to sitting is worse. While bad enough, to hear ungodly counsel is not as bad as standing in the lifestyle in which sinners stand. But neither of them is as bad as sitting as a scorner of all that is godly. That regressive seat of the scornful is precisely where the walk and the stand are intended by the enemy of our souls to leave us.

As the ankles are used to walk and the knees are used to stand, the waist is that with which we sit. So it is no wonder Ezekiel is then directed to walk further into the Spirit River until his waist was immersed.

It is interesting that it is our loins (the term used in the King James Version) wherein our faculties of reproduction reside, and the seat of the scornful *reproduces* the same sort of scorn from our lives that first manifested from others as the first regressive step in ungodly counsel. The regressive cycle then occurs towards others through us! Oh, how we need to see the Spirit influence us instead!

Comparing Psalm 1 with Ezekiel 47 causes us to see a contrast of what influences our lives – fleshly influence or influence of God's Spirit.

MEASURING THE SPIRIT RIVER OF LIFE

WATERS TO SWIM IN

Finally, one last measurement of a thousand more cubits, brought Ezekiel four thousand cubits into the River, and caused him to come to the dimension of *swimming*.

When we compare Psalm 1, where the negative side of the picture shows a person's need to not walk, stand nor sit in such wicked states of being, the wicked are then contrasted from the righteous in a fourth phase.

> *Psalms 1:3-5 And he shall be like a tree planted by the rivers of water, that bringeth forth his fruit in his season; his leaf also shall not wither; and whatsoever he doeth shall prosper. The ungodly are not so: but are like the chaff which the wind driveth away. Therefore the ungodly shall not stand in the judgment, nor sinners in the congregation of the righteous.*

THE RIVER OR THE WIND – TREES OR CHAFF?

Instead of **the River** of the Spirit taking Ezekiel away, as the prophet's feet lifted off the floor of the river, **the wind** blows the wicked away like chaff!

After Ezekiel swam in the river, he looked and suddenly saw trees on either side of the river whose leaves were for healing and fruit was bountiful every month.

> *Ezekiel 47:6-7 And he said unto me, Son of man, hast thou seen this? Then he brought me, and caused me to return to the brink of the river. Now when I had returned, behold, at the bank of the river were very many trees on the one side and on the other.*

Similarly, David spoke of the righteous who are not blown away with wind but instead remain immovable. They are so solid and stationary that they are as trees planted by the river! In light of this, consider how Adam saw the Tree of Life as well as the Tree of the Knowledge of Good and Evil in the Garden. But when we read Revelation 22, there is no Tree of Knowledge, just the Tree of Life! This speaks of people whose lives became the planting of the Lord and trees of righteousness (Isa. 61:3), while the wicked are removed from the scene forevermore.

The ungodly shall not be able to stand and remain in the judgment. After the White Throne judgment in Revelation 20, we read of Trees of Life standing aside both sides of the River.

No wonder John heard a cry for those who are thirsty to come and drink of the waters of life that they may live forever!

> *Revelation 22:17 And the Spirit and the bride say, Come. And let him that heareth say, Come. And let him that is athirst come. And whosoever will, let him take the water of life freely.*

We can drink of this river of God's Spirit in order to affect those areas of our lives that would otherwise walk in ungodly counsel, stand in the lifestyle of sinners, and sit in the seat of the scornful. If we can allow the man with the measuring line, Jesus, to show us how the Spirit works and relate to us the Law of this Spirit through His personal example on earth, we will remain in this Kingdom forevermore! Jesus lived a life of being empowered by the Spirit. In that manner, He stood as the man with the measuring line in His hand. His life taught us what to do.

IN THE RIVER AND THE RIVER IN YOU

Ezekiel swam in the River whose banks produced Trees of life with leaves for healing and fruit for meat. John was told people can drink of that same river. Ezekiel got himself in the River and John heard about getting the River inside himself. It's like saying, "Abide in me and I in you," when Jesus spoke of coming into perfect union with His Spirit (John 15:4) to produce "much fruit" (John 15:5).

19

THE ARMOUR OF GOD

Ephesians 6:11-13 Put on the whole armour of God, that ye may be able to stand against the wiles of the devil. For we wrestle not against flesh and blood, but against principalities, against powers, against the rulers of the darkness of this world, against spiritual wickedness in high places. Wherefore take unto you the whole armour of God, **that ye may be able to withstand in the evil day, and having done all, to stand.**

Notice the emphasis upon *standing*. We do not fall like a house on the sand, but we are meant to stand. Peter said we must add seven things to our faith so we will never fall (2 Peter 1:10), and such will administer an abundant entrance into the kingdom for us (2 Peter 1:11). Unlike the houses on sand, comprised of lives saying, "Lord, Lord," but lives that never enter this Kingdom, the seven elements of holiness actually **establish** us in the present truth (2 Peter 1:12). They make our calling and election **sure** (2 Peter 1:10).

There is an important part of the armour that is specifically emphasized in this picture of the house on the Rock. It is *the helmet of salvation.* Helmets are worn on the head, and this speaks of protecting our thoughts and minds. We have to *know* some things about *salvation* in order to withstand the attacks of the devil. The need to learn the ways of the Lord and our rights and position in Christ as believers cannot be stressed enough.

Notice that Paul wrote of the **wiles of the devil.** "Wiles" refers to the cunning arts, deceit, craft and trickery of the devil. The admonition is to be "able to stand against"... the *trickery* and *deceit* and *cunning* arts of the devil.

You shall *know* truth for that truth lets you recognize what is false. Being able to stand is something the house on the Rock enjoys. Knowing that the helmet of salvation is a very necessary piece of armour for the purpose of helping us stand, we can appreciate how *knowing* who we are in Christ is so very important.

Jesus recognized Peter's revelation of His identity from the Father, then said, "Thou art Peter."

The Rock is Jesus. It's like saying, "Since you now realize Who I am, let Me now reveal to you who you are. You are Peter and are part of the church that I will build on the Rock of Myself and My Kingdom. I am going to show you your identity, Peter, in relation to Me. Picture me as the Rock, the Son of the Living, eternal, never dying, God. That means I have power over death, Peter. You are part of the church of lively stones that I will build on My eternal, resurrection-power Life. Death will not even be able to hold you back when you are built upon and connected to Me. *Know* this revelation of your identity in Me."

So, it can be said that we wear the wonderful helmet of salvation *when we know the truth about our salvation*. This knowledge of our salvation is actually the revelation from the Son! You do not have the helmet on your head if you only have the first revelation from the Father. Those who only know the revelation from the Father call Jesus, "Lord, Lord," but do not enter the Kingdom. The helmet regards *salvation* (helmet of salvation), and salvation regards death and resurrection with Jesus Christ. Our heads or *minds* are thereby protected by such knowledge and awareness. We know who we are *in Christ*. We know who we are *on the Rock*. This is so vital in keeping our minds safe from deception. Attacks on the mind of worthlessness or inferiority and depression cannot affect the mind of a person that has a living knowledge of who they are in Christ.

THE ARMOUR OF GOD

GLORY SHINING FROM THE FACE

The idea of a helmet of protection for the *head* involves the picture of God's glory shining from one's *face*. There is a special relationship between these two thoughts. In order to see this relationship, let's go back to the time of the Exodus and the account of Moses.

Moses did not see God's glory in his day when he so desired it. God's face was hidden from Him.

> *Exodus 33:20 And he said, Thou canst not see my face: for there shall no man see me, and live.*

But even the afterglow of God's glory caused Moses to shine very brightly.

> *Exodus 34:29 And it came to pass, when Moses came down from mount Sinai with the two tables of testimony in Moses' hand, when he came down from the mount, that Moses wist not that* **the skin of his face shone while he talked with him.**

There is a controversy as to whether or not Moses allowed the light to shine from him for the people to see when he spoke to them, as opposed to Moses' veiling his face until he was done speaking to Israel. Whatever the case, Paul said the people of Israel did not realize the light on his face was actually waning and fading away. Moses kept that veil on until he went to speak to God again, where he was *rejuvenated*, so to speak, with glory to once again shine brightly.

The Septuagint version of the Old Testament (LXX) reads in Exodus 34:33 that Moses spoke to the people without the veil covering his face. When he was finished speaking, he then put the veil on. Paul seems to have alluded to that concept.

> *2 Corinthians 3:13 And not as Moses, which put a vail over his face, that the children of Israel could not stedfastly look to the end of that which is abolished:*

Jesus' glory is meant to be transferred to the people! Recall that Peter wrote in his epistle of how the truths of Christ's words are like light that shines upon us. This light continues to shine until the day dawns and the daystar arises in our hearts, leaving us shining in glory as well! This is not physical light and glory, of course, but is a picture of the spiritual glory that shines from Christ into our hearts. We, in turn, shine forth in the same glory as we are changed spiritually into the same image! In other words, we shine after Jesus shines on us.

Note in the next passage how Paul compared the Old Testament (which was done away with when Christ came) and the New Testaments as glory that shines.

> *2 Corinthians 3:11-14 For if that which is done away was glorious, much more that which remaineth is glorious. Seeing then that we have such hope, we use great plainness of speech: And not as Moses, which put a vail over his face, that the children of Israel could not stedfastly look to the end of that which is abolished: But their minds were blinded: for until this day remaineth the same vail untaken away in the reading of the old testament; which vail is done away in Christ.*

The glory of the Old Testament faded and this was represented by Moses' face losing the glory after time. The New Testament glory, however, never fades! Paul actually taught us that there was to be an end to the Old Covenant. As much as the light ceased to shine from Moses' face after a time, the Old Covenant ceased to operate when the New Covenant arrived. This greater glory of the New Covenant will never cease! "That which remaineth" is more glorious!

THE ARMOUR OF GOD

2 Corinthians 3:18 But we all, with open face beholding as in a glass the glory of the Lord, are changed into the same image from glory to glory, even as by the Spirit of the Lord.

2 Corinthians 4:6 For God, who commanded the light to shine out of darkness, hath shined in our hearts, to give the light of the knowledge of the glory of God in the face of Jesus Christ.

This glory and light is actually the knowledge of the glory of God shining from Jesus' face. This glory never fades. It changes us into the same image of Jesus Christ! Keep this thought of glory shining in one's face in mind as we continue.

THE ARMOUR AND GOD'S GLORY

There are 6 pieces of armour listed in Ephesians 6.

1. Helmet
2. Breastplate
3. Sword
4. Shield
5. Girdle
6. Shoes

See how the Lord wore these pieces of armour spiritually when He died on the cross. He fought the battle and prevailed through the death of the cross and His resurrection. He is the Captain of our salvation!

The Tabernacle of Moses was used by the writer of Hebrews chapter 9 as representing the Old Covenant. It housed 6 pieces of furniture.

Armour of God

1. Ark of the Covenant
2. Golden Altar of Incense
3. Seven Golden Candlesticks
4. Table of Shewbread
5. Laver
6. Brazen Altar

So we have six pieces of armour and six pieces of Tabernacle furniture. If we take the picture of the cross and superimpose it over a picture of the Tabernacle of Moses' layout, we can see that the positions of the 6 pieces of Tabernacle furniture correspond to the position of the locations of the 6 pieces of the armour of God on a man's body who is on a cross.

THE ARMOUR OF GOD

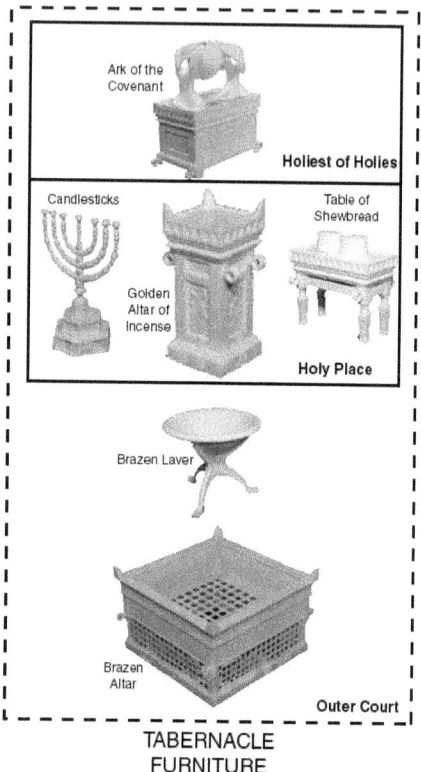

TABERNACLE FURNITURE

This means that each piece of Tabernacle furniture corresponds to a particular piece of spiritual armour.

Helmet	=	Ark of the Covenant
Breastplate	=	Golden Altar of Incense
Sword	=	Candlesticks
Shield	=	Table of Shewbread
Girdle	=	Laver
Shoes	=	Brazen Altar

Paul said we are changed into the image of Jesus Christ when we see the glory of God in the face of Jesus Christ. Contrast that with the thought of how Moses' face was veiled after he spoke to the people, and the glory faded. Similarly, all during the Old Testament period, the veil in the Tabernacle and then the Temple hid the glory of God from the face of man.

In our diagram, the part of the armour that corresponds to the Ark of the Covenant where God's glory was veiled was the Helmet of Salvation. With that in mind, consider how veiled glory represents Old Covenant administration (2 Cor. 3:13). Can you see the relationship? Moses was the spokesman for the Old Covenant. In representation of the fading glory of that covenant, Moses veiled his shining face, not allowing the people to realize that the glory shining from it was fading away. Paul used this as a spiritual picture of how the people did not realize the Old Covenant, itself, was a fading glory. It would not last forever. Even when God had the Tabernacle erected to house

THE ARMOUR OF GOD

His glory, that glory was veiled from the public eye, just like Moses' face.

But when Jesus died, that veiling that hid the glory of God in the Holiest of Holies was rent in two from the top to the bottom (Matt. 27:51)! It was as though the Face of Jesus Christ, corresponding to the placement of the veiled Ark of the Covenant, – God's glory – was unveiled forever for all to behold. His glory never fades! And it changes us, so long as we continue to gaze upon it, into His very image! Jesus is the spokesman, Himself, for the New Covenant. The glory on His face is neither veiled nor fades away. What a gloriously more perfect Covenant we have today!

> *Matthew 27:50-51 Jesus, when he had cried again with a loud voice, yielded up the ghost. (51) And, behold, the veil of the Temple was rent in twain from the top to the bottom; and the earth did quake, and the rocks rent;*

All of this contrast of glories and covenants was focused upon the death of the cross, as signified by the rending of the veil in the Temple the moment Christ died. What a work of God in the work of the cross!

You could say that this picture of the rending of the veil when Jesus died speaks a message to us that because of the cross we have come to an open access into the Holiest of Holies where the Glory of God shines in splendour!

Our *heads* are where our thinking occurs. Our minds are renewed as we learn the truths of the *glory* of the work of the cross. But our *minds* have to *accept this truth* in order for it to benefit us. We must accept it by living a life of a "self denying", "carrying our crosses" lifestyle.

When we see ourselves in union with Jesus Christ through our identification with Him on the cross – it all starts with the cross – having died with Him, been buried with Him, and even resurrected with Him, that same glory that shone from Him will shine from us! The vision of the armour of God corresponding to the six pieces of Tabernacle furniture by the layout of the cross teaches us a powerful truth. *Only in our identification with Jesus and the cross*, through not only being crucified with Him, but living a lifestyle of self-denial and carrying our crosses, *can we shine in His very image!*

Let God change you by His glory into an image of Jesus Christ. Renew your minds by the truth. Satan cannot touch your thinking with such a concept and obedient heart and conscious identification with Christ. You will not be deceived.

Jesus is bringing many sons *to glory* by showing them His glory in us! *We shine with glory* and victory as soldiers of Christ!

> *Isaiah 59:2 But your iniquities have separated between you and your God, and your sins have hid his face from you, that he will not hear.*

The face of God was hidden from us due to our sins. It was "veiled." His glory was behind the veil of the Temple and Tabernacle. We know the face of Jesus Christ is where the glory of God is found (2 Cor. 4:6). Having the knowledge of that "glory in the face of Jesus Christ" is truly knowing Him "face to face." "Face to face" is a term indicating intimacy and closeness. No man has ever seen God's face and lived (Exod. 33:20), and yet we read Moses knew God face to face (Exod. 33:11). There is no contradiction. Moses knew God intimately, though he never literally saw the face of God.

When the veil of the Temple was ripped open the moment Christ died, we see a picture of the glory of God being no longer hidden for all those who died with Christ in salvation. The sins that caused Him to hide His face from us are remitted by the blood of Jesus Christ when we are saved from sin, and the face of God is no longer hidden from us anymore. We can see His Kingdom glory and are back in fellowship with Him in the Garden Kingdom!

20

REVELATION OF
THE ARMOUR OF LIGHT

1 Peter 3:18-4:2 For Christ also hath once suffered for sins, the just for the unjust, that he might bring us to God, being put to death in the flesh, but quickened by the Spirit: By which also he went and preached unto the spirits in prison; Which sometime were disobedient, when once the longsuffering of God waited in the days of Noah, while the ark was a preparing, wherein few, that is, eight souls were saved by water. The like figure whereunto even baptism doth also now save us (not the putting away of the filth of the flesh, but the answer of a good conscience toward God,) by the resurrection of Jesus Christ: Who is gone into heaven, and is on the right hand of God; angels and authorities and powers being made subject unto him. Forasmuch then as Christ hath suffered for us in the flesh, **arm yourselves likewise with the same mind:** *for he that hath suffered in the flesh hath ceased from sin; That he no longer should live the rest of his time in the flesh to the lusts of men, but to the will of God.*

Peter related to us a comparison of ourselves with Jesus Christ for the purpose of showing us the overall truth that we have power in the Kingdom of God. It is related to the understanding of the armour of God.

SALVATION BY THE RESURRECTION OF JESUS

Notice that Peter first mentioned how Christ suffered in the flesh but was quickened by the Spirit. This is a very important point. He then went on to speak about Noah's ark, the flood, and how we can see a pattern of salvation in that story. He indicated that as water saved Noah and his family, water baptism saves us by the resurrection of Jesus. We then read Jesus resurrected and went into Heaven to the right hand throne. He is presently in authority over angels, authorities, and powers. This present dominion of Jesus Christ is mentioned for a very specific reason. It has something to do with our salvation *by the resurrection of Jesus*. The same resurrection that placed Him on the throne saved us. But it didn't just save us.

"ARM" YOURSELF WITH THIS UNDERSTANDING AND CEASE FROM SIN

Chapter 4 of Peter's epistle continues the thought. As much as Christ suffered in the flesh, we are told to *arm ourselves with the same mind*. There is a certain mindset, or understanding, that is actually considered to be *armour* by Peter!

The reason we should arm ourselves with the same mind of Christ is provided by Peter. He said that suffering in the flesh was not something that only Jesus could experience. Every true believer enjoys a special union with Christ's suffering. That is the reason we can arm ourselves with the same understanding. Those who suffer in the flesh, as Jesus did, are said to cease from sin.

This is precisely what Paul taught in the book of Romans.

> *Romans 6:6 Knowing this, that our old man is crucified with him, that the body of sin might be destroyed, that henceforth we should not serve sin.*

We suffered in the flesh by sheer virtue of the fact that our baptism into Jesus Christ caused us to claim His experience of dying as our own. We died with Jesus Christ by faith. As far as God is concerned, when Jesus died we died. The experience of suffering in the flesh has already occurred for everyone who was baptized into Jesus Christ. His death became our deaths.

> *Romans 6:3 Know ye not, that so many of us as were baptized into Jesus Christ were baptized into his death?*

Since we were united to His death in our baptism, and He suffered in the flesh in that suffering, then we can say we suffered in the flesh with Christ. If those who suffer in the flesh cease from sin, then we have come into the position of cessation from sin. We have that status! However, as any one of us can attest, that does not mean we automatically had victory over sin and have never sinned since our salvation. So how can it be that we were in such a position of victory over sin and yet have sinned? The answer lies in Peter's words. We must arm ourselves with that understanding, or else this position we hold does us no good.

GET THIS BELOW OUR COLLAR BONES AND INTO OUR HEARTS

The truth of our co-deaths with Christ requires a revelatory experience for us to truly appreciate it and benefit from it. Arming ourselves with that understanding is actually getting a revelation of it. We can know about it and quote the scriptures that state it. But as my pastor used to say, when it gets below our collar bones and into our hearts, we can truly appreciate it.

As soon as we receive revelation of this truth, the armour is on us! No enemy can stand against us and see us fall. How can we be defeated if we *know* about the power that we have going for us? This truth cannot be enjoyed in practical life every day unless we have *faith in it*. This is because the Spirit cannot work on our behalves and anoint us with such power without our faith for Him to do so.

Peter taught that ceasing from sin awards us the privilege of not having to live the rest of our lives to the lusts of the flesh.

> *1 Peter 4:1-2 Forasmuch then as Christ hath suffered for us in the flesh, arm yourselves likewise with the same mind: for he that hath suffered in the flesh hath ceased from sin; That he no longer should live the rest of his time in the flesh to the lusts of men, but to the will of God.*

Our heritage is to live free of the bondage to fulfilling the lusts of the flesh! Praise God! What a position of victory!

> *Romans 6:6-7 Knowing this, that our old man is crucified with him, that the body of sin might be destroyed, that henceforth we should not serve sin. For he that is dead is freed from sin.*

Paul emphasized our need to *know* this truth. Be aware of it. Comprehend it. Once we *know* it, we can act upon it. We arm ourselves with it.

Arming ourselves with this understanding makes it *real for us*. It is real, nevertheless. But unless *it is real to us* we cannot benefit from it, since we will not expect to enjoy such a position if we really do not believe we have it. Making something real is *realizing* it. As much as "immortalizing" a thing means that something is made immortal, "realizing" something is making it real. We must **realize** that we are dead to sin and freed from it.

LIKEWISE, WE ARE DEAD TO SIN

Paul explained that we must reason that whatever happened to Jesus can be understood as being true for us due to our union to Him. Read carefully how Paul walks us through this concept.

> *Romans 6:8-11 Now if we be dead with Christ, we believe that we shall also live with him: Knowing that Christ being raised from the dead dieth no more; death hath no more dominion over him. For in that he died, he died unto sin once: but in that he liveth, he liveth unto God. Likewise reckon ye also yourselves to be dead indeed unto sin, but alive unto God through Jesus Christ our Lord.*

As much as Jesus resurrected and had power over sin, we must *realize* this to be true of ourselves. We are as much dead to sin and alive to God as Jesus is! When verse 11 used the term "likewise," it indicated that whatever was true of Jesus as noted in verses 9 and 10 is identically true of us. Since He died to sin once, we are dead indeed to sin. Since he is alive to God forevermore, we are alive to God. It is all true *through Jesus Christ.* We connected to all of this to be able to benefit from it when we were first baptized into His death.

As a royal conclusion to this wonderful union, Paul stated something Peter also mentioned:

> *Romans 6:12 Let not sin therefore reign in your mortal body, that ye should obey it in the lusts thereof.*

> *1 Peter 4:2 That he no longer should live the rest of his time in the flesh to the lusts of men, but to the will of God.*

Because we died with Christ to sin, and are therefore freed from sin, we do not need to let sin rule in our mortal bodies. What a miracle! Think about it. Our bodies are still mortal, but they do not have to be the containers of a wicked ruler called sin. While we still have mortal bodies, we can live as Jesus Christ lives since His resurrection in an immortal body!

REVELATION OF THE ARMOUR OF LIGHT

LIVING IN MORTAL BODIES, BUT ENJOYING VICTORY OVER SIN

Jesus resurrected in a very immortal body. He bore wounds that formerly killed that body, as He revealed Himself to His disciples. Ever since that immortal resurrection, he "liveth unto God" (Romans 6:10). Paul said we can actually enjoy the same victory over sin as Jesus does in His immortal body while we still have mortal bodies.

At this point, everyone is asking, "Well, *how* is this enjoyed? If this is true, then how do we experience it?"

Paul gave the answer. In my own personal search through Paul's teachings, looking for the answer of answers to this question, I came to realize the next verse lays it out.

> *Romans 6:13 Neither yield ye your members as instruments of unrighteousness unto sin: but yield yourselves unto God, as those that are alive from the dead, and your members as instruments of righteousness unto God.*

Once we *know* this truth, *reckon* or realize it to be true of ourselves, we must then *yield* ourselves to God as people who know we are dead to sin and alive to God. The revelation of this is the reckoning of it – the realization of it. Once we get this revelation, we go straight to the Lord in prayer! We present ourselves in prayer to God as people who are alive from the dead. We have the awareness that we are indeed dead to sin and therefore freed from sin. We need only go to God with this faith and pray for Him to use our bodily members – our arms, legs, hands, mouths – as His instruments of righteousness. When our bodily members are called His instruments that means He utilizes them and works through them as we would use any given instrument in our hands.

We are not rendered into robots as though He begins to use us like a puppet to ensure we do good deeds, but we *cooperate* with His leading. We have no need to wonder how we can cooperate with Him, because *we will know that we know how* when it happens.

LET NOT SIN RULE, BUT LET THE SPIRIT EMPOWER

So, instead of seeing sin rule in our mortal bodies, we will see the Spirit empower our mortal bodies! This is precisely what Paul said, too!

> *Romans 8:11-12 But if the Spirit of him that raised up Jesus from the dead dwell in you, he that raised up Christ from the dead shall also quicken your mortal bodies by his Spirit that dwelleth in you. Therefore, brethren, we are debtors, not to the flesh, to live after the flesh.*

Many think this refers to a physical resurrection of our bodies, but it actually is not. The reason I know this is due to what the 12th verse says. We can experience the quickening, or enlivening, of our *mortal bodies* by the Spirit that resurrected Jesus from the grave *so that we do not have to live after the flesh any more*. We know that after our physical bodies are resurrected that we shall not have a worry of living after the flesh. This can only refer to our lives within mortal bodies. For that reason Paul said the Spirit will quicken our *mortal bodies*. Compare these two passages together to get the full picture.

> *Romans 8:11-12 But if the Spirit of him that raised up Jesus from the dead dwell in you, he that raised up Christ from the dead shall also quicken your mortal bodies by his Spirit that dwelleth in you.* **Therefore, brethren, we are debtors, not to the flesh, to live after the flesh.**

> *1 Peter 4:1-2 Forasmuch then as Christ hath suffered for us in the flesh, arm yourselves likewise with the same mind: for*

> *he that hath suffered in the flesh hath ceased from sin;* **That he no longer should live the rest of his time in the flesh to the lusts of men, but to the will of God.**

Now, compare these two passages, and see they are contrasting sin ruling our mortal bodies with the Spirit quickening our mortal bodies:

> *Romans 6:11-12 Likewise reckon ye also yourselves to be dead indeed unto sin, but alive unto God through Jesus Christ our Lord.* **Let not sin therefore reign in your mortal body, that ye should obey it in the lusts thereof.**

> *Romans 8:11-12 But if the Spirit of him that raised up Jesus from the dead dwell in you, he that raised up Christ from the dead* **shall also quicken your mortal bodies** *by his Spirit that dwelleth in you. Therefore, brethren, we are debtors, not to the flesh, to live after the flesh.*

Instead of seeing sin *rule in our mortal bodies*, let us see the Spirit *quicken our mortal bodies*. This quickening is an empowering! Read these scriptures until the knowledge becomes a revelation – until it gets below your collar bone – and then present yourself to the Spirit of God for quickening. This is how we arm ourselves with the knowledge of our position in Christ so that we stop living after the lusts of men.

HIS DEATH LED TO HIS RESURRECTION, AND OUR RESURRECTIONS!

Now we know why Peter said baptism saves us by the resurrection of Jesus. Baptism accomplished in faith connects us and puts us into the very death of Jesus Christ. Since His death caused Him to die to sin and live to God, and we died with Him, then we died to sin. It's not the water in water baptism that actually does anything, but it is the faith we exert in knowing we died with Christ and are buried with Him by baptism into that death (Romans 6:4). This was accomplished so we could enjoy the benefits of the resurrection Jesus Christ experienced.

> *Romans 6:5 For if we have been planted together in the likeness of his death, we shall be also in the likeness of his resurrection:*

Again, this is not speaking of a resurrection of the body that we have not yet experienced, although I believe that will occur at the Lord's coming. This resurrection is a spiritual one in which we can enjoy the victory Jesus had over sin while we still live in mortal bodies.

The death Jesus experienced that led Him to His resurrection into such glory and dominion is counted as our own deaths. This was so that we could likewise enjoy the same victory over sin that He presently enjoys. Hence, baptism saves us by the resurrection of Jesus. In other words, immersion into His death that causes us to share His death causes us to also share the victory over sin that He experienced. That means we do not have to live after the lusts of men any more!

Paul told us to *know* this truth. Peter informs us that it is an armour!

PUT ON THE ARMOUR BY PUTTING ON CHRIST

Picture yourself in a position over sin with absolute power over it, but you are not enjoying it nor even believing it is true. Then you receive teaching about it and begin to understand and believe in it. It suddenly hits you that the same experiences of Jesus are true of you due to your union to Him, then you have the same power over sin that He has! With that newfound awareness, the revelation hits you and grabs you! You then go to the Lord and pray saying you finally realize this is true of you, and you ask Him to empower and anoint you with His strength to overcome sin. That is what I call arming ourselves with armour!

> *Romans 13:12-14 The night is far spent, the day is at hand: let us therefore cast off the works of darkness, and* **let us put on the armour of light.** *Let us walk honestly, as in the day; not in rioting and drunkenness, not in chambering and wantonness, not in strife and envying. But* **put ye on the Lord Jesus Christ, and make not provision for the flesh, to fulfil the lusts thereof.**

Putting on the armour of light is the same thing as putting on the Lord Jesus Christ. It is becoming conscious of the fact that Christ's experiences of death and resurrection are our own. That means we have power over sin. Notice that Paul noted the same powerful point that Peter did. "Make not provision for the flesh, to fulfil the lusts thereof." Peter said, "baptism saves us by the resurrection of Jesus… That he no longer should live the rest of his time in the flesh to the lusts of men, but to the will of God."

This truly is dominion and Garden Kingdom power!

CLOTHED WITH ARMOUR OF LIGHT

They say Adam was clothed with light, disabling him from noticing his nakedness and being made ashamed of it. The robes of linen in Revelation represent the righteousness of the saints. After Adam sinned, this robe of light and glory vanished, and he saw his nudity and was ashamed. If this is true, consider the thought that God restored us to Garden Kingdom glory, clothing us in **armour of light** so we need not suffer a blow from the devil to fall us as it did Adam. We are protected! Knowing who we are, and being convinced of it in revelatory understanding, arms us and keeps us from deception and its subsequent victory over us.

Now we can appreciate what it means to have the helmet of salvation. We *know* we are saved and how we were saved, and this protects our minds from deception! How can we be deceived when we *know* we are saved from sin and have understood it clearly? Then there is the breastplate of righteousness. As soon as we grasp this revelation and present ourselves to God for empowerment, we immediately wear this breastplate. The breastplate protects all the major organs of the body. Everything major about our salvation is protected by His righteousness. No wonder Paul said we put on the Lord Jesus when he said we put on the armour of light! ***He is*** our righteousness!

Our feet are shod with the preparation of the Gospel, and we **walk out** this status and position of being dead, buried and risen into power with Jesus. Our belt is truth! It holds it all together. What truth we have when we know our position in Christ!

Then, of course, there is the shield of faith and the sword of the Spirit, the Word of God. The weapons of our warfare are spiritual! We use this truth as a weapon to defeat lies and even demons that attack us, as Jesus used the Word when the devil tempted Him in the wilderness. The faith we now have upon receiving this revelation is enough of a shield anyone might wish to have against our enemy.

As soon as we grasp this truth in true revelation – BOOM! – we are covered in armour of light. We are duly armed, and no weapon formed against us shall prosper (Isa. 54:17)! This is what it means to put on Christ. Not only do we have power over demons, but we have power over the sins of the flesh. Going forth with this revelation and understanding is what is called "walking after the Spirit."

Galatians 5:16 This I say then, Walk in the Spirit, and ye shall not fulfil the lust of the flesh.

REVELATION OF THE ARMOUR OF LIGHT

Arm Yourselves With the Same Mind

Peter said Christ's resurrection caused Him to be seated on the Right Hand throne of power over angels, authorities and powers. Christ understood this when He suffered and died for us. He knew He would come to that place of Kingdom power. The most oft-quoted Old Testament verse referenced in the New Testament is the following passage:

> *Psalms 110:1-2 A Psalm of David. The LORD said unto my Lord, Sit thou at my right hand, until I make thine enemies thy footstool. The LORD shall send the rod of thy strength out of Zion: rule thou in the midst of thine enemies.*

This was what Christ was told when He sat down at that right hand throne. That was the mind of Christ, so to speak. Therefore, if we are told to arm ourselves with the same mind, we can apply that statement made by the Father to the Son to our own lives. We can claim the truth that God told us to sit at the right hand throne in Christ until our enemies are made our footstool. We can place our stakes in the truth that the rod of our strength shall be sent out of Zion and we shall rule in the midst of our enemies! This understanding given to Christ is the understanding and "the mind" with which we must arm ourselves.

Praise God! Let's truly enjoy this Garden Kingdom under our glorious Last Man Adam, Jesus Christ!

21

VINDICATION OF THE PRIESTHOOD

God initially promised everyone in Israel that they would be a Kingdom of priests.

Exodus 19:5-6 Now therefore, if ye will obey my voice indeed, and keep my covenant, then ye shall be a peculiar treasure unto me above all people: for all the earth is mine: And **ye shall be unto me a kingdom of priests***, and an holy nation. These are the words which thou shalt speak unto the children of Israel.*

But before Moses could give them the tablets of the Ten Commandments, everyone broke the very first commandment! They worshiped a golden calf, transgressing the command to worship the Lord and none else. Moses cried for those on the Lord's side to come and stand with him. The tribe of Levi separated themselves from the idolaters and stood beside Moses.

God did not forget that act of dedication. That day was actually the day of Pentecost according to Jewish tradition. People were made priests that day, just as the day of Pentecost in Acts 2 brought the power of the Holy Ghost upon the people and made them kings and priests (Acts 1:8; 2:1-4)!

Time passed and a dispute arose between Korah and Moses. Korah felt that all of them could minister. He gathered Dathan,

VINDICATION OF THE PRIESTHOOD

Abiram plus 250 men of renown to protest against Moses' leadership.

Moses commanded them to stand apart from everyone else, and the earth swallowed up Korah's family in judgment, and fire smote the 250 with him.

The next day Israel continued to complain against Moses as though it was his fault for the destruction. Then God established the identity of the tribal priesthood with a sign that would remain with them from that time forward.

Moses told the people to take the staffs from their tribal princes with each tribal prince's name etched in their respective rods, with his brother Aaron's name on the tribal staff for Levi.

> *Numbers 17:7-8 And Moses laid up the rods before the LORD in the tabernacle of witness. And it came to pass, that on the morrow Moses went into the tabernacle of witness; and, behold, the rod of Aaron for the house of Levi was budded, and brought forth buds, and bloomed blossoms, and yielded almonds.*

Moses put these rods in the most holy place before the Ark of the Covenant, or "Ark of the Testimony" as it was also called. Overnight, of all the twelve rods, the rod of Aaron alone was transformed from a dead stick of wood into a resurrected branch of an almond tree. However, this was more than a living branch. It simultaneously bore buds, flowers and almonds! Natural branches only bear each of these three elements one at a time. This was supernatural life!

Branches cannot bear buds at the same time that they bear flowers and almonds. After the bud appears, it turns into the flower, and then after the flower grows the fruit or almond nut.

MORE ALMOND BRANCHES

The almond branch supernaturally bearing buds, flowers and almonds is seen elsewhere in the Bible.

> *Exodus 25:31-33 And thou shalt make a candlestick of pure gold: of beaten work shall the candlestick be made: his shaft, and his branches, his bowls, his knops, and his flowers, shall be of the same. And six branches shall come out of the sides of it; three branches of the candlestick out of the one side, and three branches of the candlestick out of the other side: Three bowls made like unto almonds, with a knop and a flower in one branch; and three bowls made like almonds in the other branch, with a knop and a flower: so in the six branches that come out of the candlestick.*

The seven golden candlesticks, or Tabernacle Menorah (like a candelabra), was identical in its description of Aaron's resurrected rod. Its knops were the buds. It had flowers. It was also to be made with bowls that were shaped like almonds. These depict the three stages of growth on the almond branch.

The kind of life that was required to not only resurrect a dead almond branch, but to also simultaneously cause it to grow three consecutive stages of growth, is eternal Life. This reminds us of the Tree of Life in the Garden of Eden.

A Connecting Vision Involving the Candlesticks

When Jesus appeared to John in the first chapter of Revelation, He was seen standing in the midst of seven candlesticks.

> *Revelation 1:13 And in the midst of the seven candlesticks one like unto the Son of man, clothed with a garment down to the foot, and girt about the paps with a golden girdle.*

VINDICATION OF THE PRIESTHOOD

Only two elements from this overall vision of Jesus were interpreted for us. One of them was the set of candlesticks.

> *Revelation 1:20 The mystery of the seven stars which thou sawest in my right hand, and the seven golden candlesticks. The seven stars are the angels of the seven churches: and the seven candlesticks which thou sawest are the seven churches.*

When we picture Jesus standing in the middle of these candlesticks, He is standing amidst the churches symbolically. Such a vision shows Him as though the branches actually protrude from His sides. This corresponds to His teachings.

> *John 15:5* **I am the vine, ye are the branches:** *He that abideth in me, and I in him, the same bringeth forth much fruit: for without me ye can do nothing.*

The point Jesus made in speaking of us as branches connected to Him was that we cannot produce anything of any spiritual value without His Life working in us. His Life is resurrection Life. This is precisely what we require in order to be priests unto God. We must actually live of Him (John 6:57).

Just as the rod of Aaron simultaneously bore buds, flowers and fruit in resurrection Life in order to prove Aaron's priesthood, the candlesticks bear the same emblems.

In Revelation chapter 2's first letter that was written to the Ephesian Church, which one of the seven candlesticks signified, Jesus introduced Himself with a specific description of Himself from Chapter 1's vision. In fact, each of the seven letters to the churches begins with a different part of Chapter 1's vision of Jesus. The particular element of the vision is chosen in each letter's introduction with the situation of that specific Church in mind.

> *Revelation 2:1 Unto the angel of the church of Ephesus write; These things saith he that holdeth the seven stars in his right hand, who walketh in the midst of the seven golden candlesticks;*

Beginning this letter with the very two elements of the vision that were interpreted for us, the Lord is implying an important truth to this Church. As the Candlesticks are positioned as branches coming forth from the Lord, something is then said to this Church that is related to what Jesus explained concerning branches that abide in Himself, the Vine.

> *Revelation 2:5 Remember therefore from whence thou art fallen, and repent, and do the first works; or else I will come unto thee quickly, and* **will remove thy candlestick out of his place**, *except thou repent.*

As one of the candlesticks amongst which Jesus stands, this Church was expected to perform a vital function in the Kingdom. Failure to perform that function would warrant the removal of their candlestick. Think of the Candlesticks as Branch-shaped lampstands as we read Christ's words in John's Gospel.

> *John 15:5-6 I am the vine, ye are the branches: He that abideth in me, and I in him, the same bringeth forth much fruit: for without me ye can do nothing.* **If a man abide not in me, he is cast forth as a branch, and is**

VINDICATION OF THE PRIESTHOOD

withered*; and men gather them, and cast them into the fire, and they are burned.*

Abiding in the Vine of Jesus Christ causes the sap to flow from that Vine into the branch that it may bring forth fruit. Endeavouring to produce fruit of its own accord without attachment to the vine is undoubtedly a futile effort on the part of any given branch. However, this is just what many Christians do all the time, and do not even realize it. When self-life tries to accomplish a work for God without reliance upon the Spirit within, we are not abiding in the vine and relying upon the Life of the vine to originate the fruit. Abiding in the Vine is reliance upon the Life of the vine. It is worrying only about being connected to that Vine so the Life may flow from it and into the branches. Imagine a branch trying its best to produce fruit without attachment to the Vine.

The Lord said that such a branch will be removed from the Vine and cast into the fire. Similarly, since Jesus was in the midst of the branch-shaped Candlesticks, failure for this Church to thrive upon the Resurrection Life of Jesus in order to accomplish His will would warrant the removal of their Candlestick as Adam was removed from the Garden.

Notice what it was that caused the need for the Church's warning.

> *Revelation 2:2-4 I know thy works, and thy labour, and thy patience, and how thou canst not bear them which are evil: and thou hast tried them which say they are apostles, and are not, and hast found them liars: And hast borne, and hast patience, and for my name's sake hast laboured, and hast not fainted. Nevertheless I have somewhat against thee, because thou hast left thy first love.*

It was not a lack of works and accomplishments that endangered this Church's Candlestick. It was a matter of those works being accomplished in fleshly power, and not the offspring birthed from a relationship with the Lord. When the Lord originates a work, it is because of His Spirit working through the Church. They lost their *first love*.

The work of the Lord is intended to be a reproduction through the Church in much the same way a woman bears a child for her husband. Relationship between a man and his wife is responsible for reproduction. It is relationship that occurs when a Branch abides in the Vine.

When the resurrected Almond Branch of Levi's tribe manifested buds, flowers and fruit, it was doing so as the result of unnatural Life within it. Resurrection Life. This proved the Priesthood of Levi.

This is exactly what the Apostle Paul explained as the qualification for our service to God.

> *Romans 6:13 Neither yield ye your members as instruments of unrighteousness unto sin: but yield yourselves unto God, as those that are alive from the dead, and your members as instruments of righteousness unto God.*

The absolute need for life from the dead is what it takes for us to be able to present ourselves before God that we might minister in His Kingdom.

We must present ourselves to God in this fashion and with this understanding. Was it not before the Ark of the Covenant, before the presence of God, where the tribal rods of Israel were presented in order to prove the priesthood? Resurrection Life was the qualification.

Putting this thought together with the concept of the Most Holy Place standing as a model of the Garden of Eden allows the picture to have even more full meaning. Jesus came that we might have more abundant Life that we lost upon banishment. Resurrection Life is restored supernatural Life of God that was intended to course through our beings had Adam not sinned and abrogated his opportunity with the Tree of Life.

But the wonderful picture does not stop there.

VINDICATION OF THE PRIESTHOOD

THE TOMB OF JESUS WAS IN A GARDEN

John 19:41-42 Now in the place where he was crucified there was a garden; and in the garden a new sepulchre, wherein was never man yet laid. There laid they Jesus therefore because of the Jews' preparation day; for the sepulchre was nigh at hand.

Jesus Christ was prophesied as the Branch (Isa. 11:1; Zech. 3:8). Like the dead almond branch of Aaron's rod laid in the most holy place, Jesus was laid as dead in a Garden. The Most Holy Place represented the Garden of Eden. Supernatural Life brought the deceased Branch back from the dead and He became High Priest. But His priesthood goes beyond that of Levi. In this priesthood, all of us are priests and we are all meant to enter into the Most Holy Place, whereas Levi's priesthood only allowed the High Priest to come before the Lord.

Hebrews 9:12 Neither by the blood of goats and calves, but by his own blood he entered in once into the holy place, having obtained eternal redemption for us.

Hebrews 10:19 Having therefore, brethren, boldness to enter into the holiest by the blood of Jesus,

We enter the Most Holy Place by the same means Jesus Christ did. His blood!

It might seem contradictory to learn that Paul taught life from the dead as the qualification for entrance into God's presence in spiritual priesthood, whereas we read in Hebrews 10 that possession of the Blood of Jesus is our way in. However, the single truth comes forth in both scenarios.

Before the Cross, the High Priest carried the blood the atonement sacrifice into the Holiest of Holies. This can hardly be viewed as resurrection. However, what else could be done in order to foreshadow Christ's future resurrection? Christ would be both the sacrifice for Atonement as well as the High Priest offering the blood of that Sacrifice. In order for Him to be able to shed His blood in death and then present it in the most Holy Place, He would have to resurrect from the dead!

Since His death, burial and resurrection were enjoined to us as our own deaths, burials and resurrections with Him by the Gospel, we hereby realize the significance. He went in with His own blood and we likewise enter in with His blood. His blood that was presented in the Holiest of Holies stood as proof of both His resurrection and our own. And Resurrection Life is the qualification for Priesthood!

As the Life of the Vine flows into the branch, Christ's death is claimed as our own deaths. His burial is our burial. His resurrection is also our own. Christ died once to sin, and ever lives unto God as High Priest. Likewise, we died once indeed to sin, and are alive forevermore through Jesus Christ (Rom. 6:10-11). The supernatural Life within the resurrected Almond Branch depicts all of this truth.

The whole scenario points us to Garden of Eden restoration. We belong in the Garden Kingdom. In fact, the Almond Branch was taken back into the Garden's model of the Most Holy Place and stored in the Ark of the Covenant for safe keeping. It stood as an ever-present reminder that the family of Aaron was the priesthood.

Kings, But Priests As Well

We seem to easily understand our status as Kings in the Kingdom. Kings command, dominate and conquer. Kings are people of power. But what about our Priesthood? Priesthood is ministry unto others. This requires supernatural Life flowing in and through us so that others may be administered to.

Many hesitate in thinking of themselves as useful ministers for God. They think they are inadequate. The qualities they assume they require in order to have confidence to present themselves before God in His Most Holy presence are lacking in their estimation. However, Paul made it abundantly clear that the real qualification for ministry is Life from the dead. Resurrection Life. This is something that we cannot engineer nor contrive. We simply require an experience of true salvation wherein God raises us to walk in newness of Life through New Birth.

In fact, if we assume we can be used by God because of any reason aside from life from the dead, we are legalists whose flesh strives to make itself useful to God through natural life.

His resurrection alone makes us worthy to be useful to God as His ministers in His wonderful Kingdom!

TAKE A BITE OF ETERNAL LIFE

With Jesus having stood amidst the seven golden candlesticks that were shaped like Almond branches, we see a Garden-like picture. It's like the Tree of Life with supernatural Life manifested within. As the first letter to the seven churches depicted this Edenic scene, the first "age" of mankind involved the Garden of Eden and the Tree of Life.

Should the Ephesian Church overcome their predicament, note the reward. They could *Take a Bite of Eternal Life!*

> *Revelation 2:7 He that hath an ear, let him hear what the Spirit saith unto the churches; To him that overcometh will I give to eat of the tree of life, which is in the midst of the paradise of God.*

Appendix

A Miracle of Confirmation!

I had prayed for confirmation from the Lord by way of a sign concerning where my next step in ministry should take me. I knew I was to relocate from my current location, but did not know where. A fellow minister agreed with me to pray for God to give me a sign concerning direction. There were two doors open to me. One in Texas and the other in California, and I did not know which to take. So, I left it in the hands of the Lord, expecting the sign I prayed for to come to pass whenever God chose fit to do so.

While on a flight from Winnipeg to California to minister in the Highland, CA, area, I was seated on my second connection in Phoenix. I boarded the plane and sat in seat B on the 22nd row, which was the middle of three seats on the left side. I watched as people walked down the aisle to find their seats, and saw a man holding my book, **Take A Bite of Eternal Life, Vol. I,** in the air in his hand! I looked twice to make sure. And sure enough, he had my book in his hand! It had just been released four months previously, and only 22 had been sold over the internet up to that point (I was in row 22).

He stopped near my row and I got up and called to him, saying, "Excuse me, you have my book." He looked at me like I was accusing him of stealing the book. I said, "I wrote that book. I am Mike Blume."

It turned out that his seat was seat "A" in my row directly beside me! God had placed our seats side by side on this plane!

I just sold the book to him online two weeks ago. He looked at my picture on the back cover and looked at me and smiled, and nodded his head. God answered my prayer!

He is a preacher – Bishop Darryl Thomas, from North

Carolina. He told me that he was invited to preach that weekend in the L.A. area. Imagine the odds of a preacher from North Carolina connecting on the same flight as my final connection to California from Winnipeg, seated side by side with me and holding one of only 22 books I sold worldwide in his hand!

He could have kept the book in his suitcase, hidden from view, but he was holding it up in the air in his hand looking for his seat. There I was on a trip to one of the two options opened to me, after praying for a sign to confirm which one I should take, and this happened!

What a time of fellowship with the good Bishop that we had over the wonders of the Lord during that flight!

The man beside me on the seat "C" overheard our conversation and was amazed. I asked him to take our picture.

Mike Blume with Bishop Darryl Thomas
May 1, 2007

www.ingramcontent.com/pod-product-compliance
Lightning Source LLC
Chambersburg PA
CBHW051044160426
43193CB00010B/1060